SCIENTISTS

AND THEIR MIND-BLOWING EXPERIMENTS

by Dr Mike Goldsmith

Illustrated by Clive Goddard

Hippo

Scholastic Children's Books,
Euston House, 24 Eversholt Street,
London NW1 1DB, UK

A division of Scholastic Ltd
London ~ New York ~ Toronto ~ Sydney ~ Auckland
Mexico City ~ New Delhi ~ Hong Kong

Published in the UK by Scholastic Ltd, 2003

10 digit ISBN 0 439 98228 6
13 digit ISBN 978 0439 98228 3

Typeset by M Rules
Printed and bound by Bookmarque Ltd, Croydon, Surrey

8 10 9

Papers used by Scholastic Children's Books are made from wood
grown in sustainable forests.

CONTENTS

INTRODUCTION

As you've probably noticed, there's an awful lot of science about these days: cars, phones, weapons of mass destruction, toothpaste – it would be a very different world without it. And, of course, everyone knows about famous scientists, their mind-blowing experiments and discoveries...

DARWIN PROVED WE'RE DESCENDED FROM MONKEYS!

EINSTEIN SAID EVERYTHING'S RELATIVE!

NEWTON EXPLAINED WHAT GRAVITY IS!

CURIE DISCOVERED RADIOACTIVITY!

AUNTIE BERYL

Yes! Exactly! Except they didn't actually do any of those things. The things they did were much more amazing...

Another thing about dead famous scientists is that most of them didn't call themselves that – the word scientist was only invented in 1833. What we think of as science – laboratories full of large-brained people, mathematics that makes your brain explode, gigantic machines that go 'Hmmmm' – only really got going in the nineteenth century.

Before that, science was only done by a few people with enquiring minds and time on their hands. Most of the dead famous scientists in this book were like that. Even though they took science seriously and knew it would one day give humanity the keys to the Universe (which you'll find in this book in handy little boxes labelled 'Secrets of Science'), most of their mates thought they were a little bit odd.

Though being a scientist is new, modern science is really just a well-organized way of doing something which people have been trying to do for thousands of years – explain the Universe, how it works and where it comes from. Many civilizations didn't get much further than saying, 'God did it' and adding, 'and don't ask how or we'll burn you alive'. But not all of them…

ARISTOTLE AND HIS MOON CREATURES

The Ancient Greeks were some of the first people to have a crack at science. Luckily, they lived in a time and place when thinking about things and questioning everything was encouraged (*if* you were male, and didn't happen to be a slave) which allowed them to speculate on all sorts of things. So that's what they did.

Not everyone calls these Ancient Greek philosophers scientists because, although they did try to explain how the world works, they tended to do it just by having a really hard think until they'd come up with a theory, and then staying up half the night getting drunk and arguing with each other about it. What they *didn't* do was to try to test their ideas by experiments or measurements or careful observations. So there was

no way to confirm or deny a theory. Hence, not surprisingly, some of them were a bit odd…

Plato, who lived a good bit after the first sort-of sciency-type Greek thinkers, set up a special academy called (rather catchily as it turned out) the Academy, in about 387 BC. The Academy was the ancestor of our universities, where philosophers could get together and have a really good old think and then a spot of lunch and a chin-wag. Twenty years later, a new pupil joined…

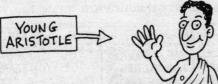

YOUNG ARISTOTLE

Aristotle really got science started. Sadly, the way he was interpreted put the brakes on again for over 1,000 years.

Warning: sorry about the lack of biographic details in this chapter. It's because there aren't many. Aristotle lived so long ago that most of the facts of his personal life have long been forgotten. About all that we know about him is that:

1. HE HAD A TRENDY HAIRCUT
2. HE HAD A NICE COLLECTION OF SHINY RINGS
3. HE WAS VERY, VERY BRAINY

And no one's completely sure about one or two. But he was *definitely* brainy, so intensely clever that Plato (a notable brainbox himself) called Aristotle 'The Mind'.

Aristotle was born in a nice little town called Stagira in northern Greece in 384 BC. Soon after, his dad got a great job as doctor to King Amyntas of Macedonia, and most of Aristotle's childhood was spent at the royal court, where he was friends with Amyntas' son, Philip. Aristotle's parents died when he was still young and, when he was 17, his guardian thought it was about time Aristotle got a proper education:

Aristotle signed up at Plato's Academy, and there he stayed for the next 20 years, first as a pupil, then as a teacher.

Teach yourself thinking

Aristotle and Plato, though very matey on the whole, didn't agree about everything. In particular, they didn't agree about how to do their jobs. Plato thought actually observing anything was beneath a good thinker and a day not spent locked in a dark room with your eyes shut having a good old think about things was a day wasted. Aristotle, on the other hand, thought the way to sort out the Universe was to look at it and *then* think about it – in other words, he thought the way to understand the world was through science, not philosophy (though he wouldn't have put it quite like that himself – in fact no one would, for thousands of years).

SECRETS OF SCIENCE

Aristotle's insistence that people should observe the world carefully before trying to explain it is about the most fundamental rule of science.

Since he was one of the first scientific-type thinkers, there was plenty for Aristotle to do. He invented physics and biology (though they were still called philosophy), revolutionized logic, and had a go at cosmology, politics, mineralogy and chemistry.

Aristotle also found time to do some sports writing and he wrote a bit about cosmetics, too.

A simpler world

I'm sure you've noticed how twinkly and nice the stars are. In ancient times, before street lighting or proper pollution had been invented, people with time on their hands must also have been impressed by the night sky and wondered why it was different from the land or the sea, what the stars were, why they moved as they did and why the constellations didn't look anything like the things they were named after.

Aristotle was one of those people, and he had a nice simple theory about what the stars were made of. And everything else too. Deciding what things were made of was a popular pursuit for thinkers in those days.

11

So as far as Aristotle was concerned, the five different types of matter (i.e. different substances) that made up the Universe were earth, air, fire, water and ether.

SECRETS OF SCIENCE

Aristotle's theory that every object is made of matter seems dead obvious now, but in those days some people thought things were made of thoughts or gods. Aristotle's matter theory meant that people were encouraged to investigate things scientifically.

Aristotle thought that the job of what we'd call a scientist was to find out the 'nature' of things. What he meant by nature is what we mean when we say 'it's in the nature of a caterpillar to grow into a butterfly' or 'it's in the nature of nettles to sting'. Aristotle tried to explain the Universe in terms of living things, all trying to live up to their natures. Non-living things had natures too – boring ones, but natures all the same. For instance, the nature of 'earth' (which included stones, metals, and other solids) was to be heavy and move towards the centre of the Earth. So if you let a bit of earth do what it 'wanted', by dropping it, it would move naturally downwards, in a straight line. Aristotle had no concept of gravity, just this idea that things 'want' to get to their natural place. As scientific principles go it was a bit rubbish, but better than nothing nevertheless.

According to Aristotle, the nature of water was to be a bit less heavy, and to lie on the surface of the Earth. The nature of air was to be lighter than earth or water, and so it took its place above the sea and land. The nature of fire was to be lighter than air, so flames flew upwards, and above the layer of the air was a fire layer with the Moon on the edge of it.

Aristotle thought earth, air, fire and water all had natural qualities to them too: earth was dry and cold, water was wet and cold, air was wet and hot and fire was dry and hot.

Left to itself, the world would be a very boring place – a sphere of earth covered entirely by an ocean, with an atmosphere around it and a fiery shell outside the atmosphere. But Aristotle thought the Sun kept everything a bit mixed-up and interesting. He also thought there was a god-like being behind it all, who had designed things to be rational, logical, orderly, and harmonious but had then pottered off to do something else, leaving the Universe running like a nice clock he'd built and wound up.

Also – what was most important – Aristotle thought human beings could understand the Universe.

SECRETS OF SCIENCE

Most early civilizations thought the Universe was a complicated, baffling place, ruled by bad-tempered and/or plain nutty gods who were completely unpredictable. The optimistic belief of the Ancient Greeks that it is actually governed by rules that humans can understand is a fundamental belief of all scientists.

People have always had a very high opinion of Aristotle, and Aristotle thought they were quite right. The words 'I don't know' were not ones that you'd hear him say (and not just because he didn't speak English). Equipped with his staggering intelligence, a few too-simple principles and a determination not to check too closely with the Universe to see if he was right, he explained *everything*.

The fifth element

Aristotle's theory explained a lot of things quite nicely:

ARISTOTLE'S SECRET
SCIENCE SCROLL

METALS MELT WHEN HEATED BECAUSE
THEY'RE MADE OF EARTH AND
WATER, AND HEATING THEM MAKES
THE WATER SHOW ITSELF.

YOU DON'T NEED TO HELP AN
APPLE FALL BECAUSE IT WANTS TO
REACH THE EARTH, BUT YOU HAVE
TO PUSH A CART ALONG BECAUSE
IT'S HAPPY WHERE IT IS.

WATER PUTS OUT FLAMES
BECAUSE OF THEIR OPPOSITE
NATURES.

But Aristotle didn't stop there. He was convinced that the Sun and stars and planets were very different from the Earth. As far as he knew, there was no change in the heavens except for some slow, regular, repetitive movements – the Sun went across the sky every day, and so did the stars and, in a more complicated way, the planets.

So Aristotle decided the stars, Sun, planets and the Moon were made of a fifth type of matter called ether. It wasn't hot, cold, dry or wet and, unlike objects below the Moon which moved naturally in straight lines, objects made of ether – like planets – moved naturally in circles. They were also supposed to last for ever. (Comets are temporary things, so they couldn't be made of ether. Aristotle decided that meant they couldn't exist beyond the Moon, and they must be in the atmosphere!)

So there we go, the Universe all nicely explained. So far, all was well. The trouble was, Aristotle didn't do what a scientist today would, which is to make some measurements, do some experiments, and calculate a few things. Science hadn't been properly invented yet, so instead he just had a good think about things. And that's where it all started to go terribly wrong:

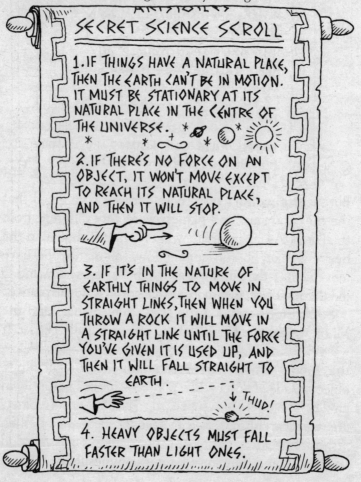

SECRET SCIENCE SCROLL

1. IF THINGS HAVE A NATURAL PLACE, THEN THE EARTH CAN'T BE IN MOTION. IT MUST BE STATIONARY AT ITS NATURAL PLACE IN THE CENTRE OF THE UNIVERSE.

2. IF THERE'S NO FORCE ON AN OBJECT, IT WON'T MOVE EXCEPT TO REACH ITS NATURAL PLACE, AND THEN IT WILL STOP.

3. IF IT'S IN THE NATURE OF EARTHLY THINGS TO MOVE IN STRAIGHT LINES, THEN WHEN YOU THROW A ROCK IT WILL MOVE IN A STRAIGHT LINE UNTIL THE FORCE YOU'VE GIVEN IT IS USED UP, AND THEN IT WILL FALL STRAIGHT TO EARTH.

THUD!

4. HEAVY OBJECTS MUST FALL FASTER THAN LIGHT ONES.

All these things are hopelessly wrong. Actually...

1. Objects fall towards the centre of the Earth, not because that's their natural place, but because they're attracted there by gravity. So there's no problem with the idea of a moving Earth.

THAT LOOKS LIKE AN ATTRACTIVE PLANET!

2. On Earth, air resistance and friction mean that you need to keep pushing some things or they'll stop — carts for instance. But you can throw an object or push it across ice and it will keep moving for some time, even though you're no longer pushing it.

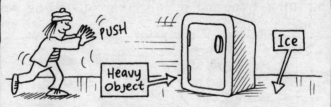

PUSH

Heavy Object

Ice

3. Thrown objects move in curves, not in straight lines.

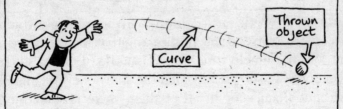

Curve

Thrown object

4. Leave this one to Galileo on page 29.

So, two out of ten for Aristotle's physics then.

Snakes and ladders

One day, after Aristotle had spent 20 years at the Academy, Plato felt a bit poorly and then:

Since Aristotle was stunningly brainy, had plenty of family cash and was only 37, he probably expected to become Mr Academy Numero Uno. But actually Plato's nephew got the job, and Aristotle went off in a huff and a boat. He went to the court of Hermeias, ruler of Atarnos. Hermeias was an ex-pupil of the Academy and Aristotle got on well with him. After a while, Aristotle married Hermeias' niece, Pythias. It's said that Aristotle spent their honeymoon collecting interesting sea-creatures.

Next, Aristotle settled down to invent zoology, which no one else fancied much, thinking that animals were a bit on the smelly and low-class side. But Aristotle reckoned 'we should approach the study of every animal without shame; for in all of them there is something natural and something beautiful'.

So Aristotle wandered about a bit in the locality, poking about in rock pools (he always loved the seaside) and observing and cutting up the animals he found there (he didn't like cutting them up really, but he forced himself to).

Aristotle was not the most observant person in the world and sometimes just believed what he was told without checking for himself. Not very scientific, I know, but I expect he was busy. For instance, he thought women had fewer teeth than men, he got the number of ribs in men wrong, and believed that the sex of a goat depended on the way the wind was blowing when it was conceived.

But Aristotle did discover some amazing things. Like: you know how when you're on a plane and your ears are blocked and you yawn, there's that funny crackling noise when your ears clear? It's because there's a tube connecting the inside of your ear with the back of your throat. Aristotle discovered this tube, though the fact was forgotten and had to be rediscovered in about 1550. He also discovered that dolphins aren't fish and that bees have a hive leader.

Aristotle didn't just investigate animals individually. He wanted to relate them to each other and classify them too. Before Aristotle's time, animals were mainly classified by the number of legs they had:

Aristotle decided to classify things according to the type of blood they had and the type of eggs they laid, if any. We still use a system a bit like this today.

The Moon creatures

Aristotle, like other Ancient Greeks, got a bit carried away with his scheme about how the Universe worked and tried to explain everything with a theory which was far too primitive. He reckoned living things were all associated with one of the four elements found on Earth – fish were watery creatures, found in the sea and rivers; plants were earthy things, found in the ground; animals and birds were airy, found in the air and sky; and the fiery creatures were, er, well … presumably they must be…

This highlights a big problem with Aristotle and the other Ancient Greek thinkers: once they had made up their minds on a theory, they would try to defend it no matter whether there was any evidence for it or not.

Back to school

After a few years spent happily poking about in rock pools and rather less happily chopping up the animals he found in them, Aristotle heard that his childhood pal Philip, now king of Macedonia, had a son whom he wanted Aristotle to teach. So Aristotle went back to Macedonia and became tutor to Alexander, aged 13. Alexander – later to be known as 'The Great' – went on to conquer half the world known to the Greeks (and to set up an enormous number of cities called 'Alexandria', which must have made travel very confusing).

It's not really known how well they got on. Alexander seems to have sent Aristotle samples of interesting plants he found from whatever bit of the world he happened to be conquering at the time, but he also wrote a letter complaining that Aristotle

ANOTHER PACKAGE FROM ALEXANDER

GREAT!

was giving public lectures on the same subjects he'd taught Alexander himself. It's hard to see why that was a problem but Alexander was a rather stroppy kind of a guy, as world conquerors tend to be.

In 335 BC, after three years of teaching, Alexander went off to do a bit more conquering, and Aristotle went back to Athens. But he was still rather cross about not being made boss of the Academy, so he decided to go to another university-type place. Unfortunately there weren't any, so he created his own and called it the Lyceum. It was a bit different from the Academy in that the people who worked there were more into maths and looking at things. And unlike the Academy it had a library and a museum.

Aristotle, and the Lyceum, became very popular for a while. In fact, most of Aristotle's surviving writings are notes for lectures at the Lyceum, which is why they tend to be a bit scribbly and scruffy.

GOOD MORNING, STUDENTS. TODAY'S LECTURE WILL BE ON... ER, HANG ON, I CAN'T READ MY OWN WRITING...

But what makes them special is how different they are from the poetic, ranting, story-based works of most earlier Greek thinkers. They're simply sequences of facts linked by logical arguments. Even though some of the facts are rather dubious and some of the arguments are a bit dodgy, it's all very modern in its tone.

Aristotle stayed happily at the Lyceum until 323 BC, when Alexander died. This was a bit of a blow to him – and it didn't do Aristotle much good either. There had always been a fair bit of anti-Macedonian feeling in Athens, and now people felt safe to do more than mutter and grumble. It was thought that Aristotle, having spent so long in Macedonia and having so many Macedonian friends, was a lot keener on Macedonia than he should be, and he was accused of being disrespectful to the gods. Something similar had happened not long before to a philosopher called Socrates, who ended up sentenced to death, so Aristotle decided not to hang around and wait for this to happen to him. He fled to Calchis where, a few months later, he died, aged 62. We don't really know how, but it's said he threw himself into the sea because he couldn't work out how the tides worked. Which just goes to show, you can be *too* keen on science.

ARISTOTLE
THAT WAS YOUR LIFE

Revolutionized:
biology, astronomy and physics

TOP DISCOVERY:
• how to be a scientist

NON-SCIENTIFIC INTERESTS:
practically everything

GALILEO GALILEI AND HIS SECRET SOLAR SYSTEM

After Aristotle's death, many other Greek thinkers followed his teachings, but most of them didn't do much more than copy his works. The contents of the Lyceum library were eventually transferred to a super new library at Alexandria, full of colour photocopiers, broadband Internet connections and glossy magazines (or their ancient equivalents). Then, in 146 BC, Greece was absorbed by the Roman Empire. The Romans were good at things like conquest and admin, but had no time for scientific thinking, so there was hardly any progress in science while they were in charge.

After the Roman Empire broke up in AD 285, everything got a bit grim and quiet in Europe and there was very little scientific progress for over 1,000 years. The Lyceum and Plato's Academy were closed and the great library at Alexandria was destroyed. However, some of Aristotle's writings survived in Arabia and in about the fifteenth century they, along with other Greek writings, were translated into Latin and became available in Europe. Everybody was *most* impressed and started to adopt Ancient Greek ideas about art and philosophy. The period was called the Renaissance, which means the rebirth.

Partly because it fitted with the Biblical idea that the Earth was the centre of the solar system, Greek science was enthusiastically adopted by the Catholic Church, which dominated Italy and many other parts of Europe. Aristotle's theories in particular, in a modified form, became official doctrine for centuries.

But while some old scientific theories were popular, the scientific *approach* – questioning, experimenting, coming up with new theories – wasn't. Questioning Aristotle wasn't quite the same as questioning the Bible – not yet – but still it was a dangerous thing to do. Anyone who wanted to take on Aristotle would have to be clever, brave, outspoken, witty and reckless, with powerful friends to protect them.

Someone like Galileo Galilei. Galileo just didn't know when to shut up.

Which was brilliant for science, but not for him...

Shouting about science

Galileo was born in Pisa, Italy, in 1564. His dad, Vincenzio, was a musician and a bit of an amateur scientist who liked to criticize Aristotle's teachings from time to time. This led to lots of arguments, which Vincenzio quite enjoyed. Galileo got at least some of his love of science, and his argumentative nature, from his dad.

When Galileo was ten, his family moved from Pisa to Florence and he went to school at a local monastery (religious institutions were a big part of life in sixteenth-century Italy). We don't know a lot about Galileo's early life, but he probably learnt religion, Latin, maths, grammar and logic at the monastery. Which all turned out to be very handy later.

After a bit, Galileo's dad decided his son should be a doctor, so Galileo was sent to Pisa University to become one. As it turned out, Galileo didn't like doctoring much and he used to sneak into the far more exciting maths lectures from time to time. He liked them so much that, encouraged by the maths lecturer, he dropped medicine and took up maths instead. He had a bit of a row with his dad about this. He had a bit of a row with most people actually, so much so that he was known as the Wrangler. The arguments were mostly about how to do science, how objects moved, and how silly it was to be made to wear a toga all the time, as students were in those days.

Swinging
Everyone else at the University thought that if you wanted to find something out – like the time it took a cannonball to fall from the top of a tower 54 metres high to the ground – the best thing to do was…

...er, no, the best way was to...

...NO! They thought the best way was to get an Aristotly old book out of the library and LOOK IT UP!

Galileo thought all explanations needed to be tested by observation and experiment. And that's what he did. One day when he was supposed to be listening to Mass in the cathedral, he noticed a lamp that had just been lit. It was swinging from side to side and gradually slowing down. Galileo didn't have a watch with him because they hadn't been invented yet, so he timed the swings with his pulse, and found that the swings seemed to last the same time whether they were wide or narrow. Instead of rushing to the library for a nice read about swinging things, he did some experiments and eventually came up with a simple mathematical law that related the length of a pendulum to the time of its swing.

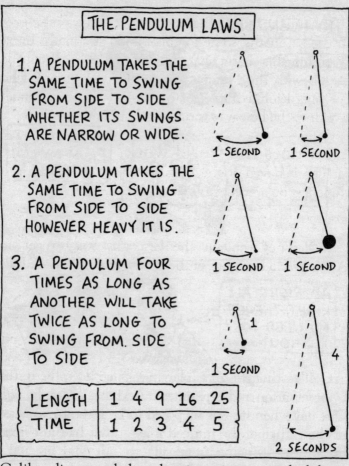

THE PENDULUM LAWS

1. A PENDULUM TAKES THE SAME TIME TO SWING FROM SIDE TO SIDE WHETHER ITS SWINGS ARE NARROW OR WIDE.

1 SECOND   1 SECOND

2. A PENDULUM TAKES THE SAME TIME TO SWING FROM SIDE TO SIDE HOWEVER HEAVY IT IS.

1 SECOND   1 SECOND

3. A PENDULUM FOUR TIMES AS LONG AS ANOTHER WILL TAKE TWICE AS LONG TO SWING FROM SIDE TO SIDE

1

1 SECOND

4

2 SECONDS

LENGTH	1	4	9	16	25
TIME	1	2	3	4	5

Galileo discovered that the time a swing took did not depend on the weight of the pendulum, which is really rather odd (and was not fully explained until Albert Einstein arrived on the scene). He also discovered what a brilliant tool maths was for describing things exactly.

In 1585, Galileo left Pisa University – with no degree. His dad couldn't afford to keep him, so he had to get a job. He went back to Florence yet again and turned on the charm. Luckily he had stacks of it and was also ever so good at maths, so he soon got a job as a maths tutor. By turning his charm up to full power, Galileo also made friends with the Marquis Guidobaldo del Monte, who got him a job as Professor of Maths – in Pisa. (Small world, eh?) The pay was rubbish, but Galileo took it.

How does the world work?

Galileo behaved at the University just as he had as a student – he argued about everything. As he said…

In questions of science, the authority of a thousand is not worth the humble reasoning of a single individual.

Not altogether surprisingly, a lot of people got a bit irritated with him. But he didn't care, he had good friends too and was enjoying himself applying his clever 'observe/measure/experiment/reason/calculate' approach to motion. (Aristotle had always said, 'To be ignorant of motion is to be ignorant of Nature,' so it was an obvious place to start.)

As we saw on page 16, Aristotle reckoned that heavy objects fall faster than light ones. Like most of Aristotle's ideas, there's something in this one – feathers fall slower than stones – but Galileo noticed that heavy and light hailstones fell together and was sure that, on the whole, objects fell at the same speed however heavy they were. He couldn't imagine that a falling object would slow down if it split up, as Aristotle predicted.

The Renaissance Review

PISA BALL-DROP SHOCK

Aristotelians are gobsmacked by unconfirmed reports from Pisa claiming that well-known bad boy of physics, Galileo Galilei, scored a major publicity coup yesterday by dropping two lead spheres from the famous Leaning Tower.

One sphere was 20 times heavier than the other so, according to Aristotle, it should have fallen 20 times faster. Yet the two spheres struck the ground almost together, closely followed by the jaws of a small crowd of Aristotelians present.

(In fact, on Earth, the resistance of the air means that objects fall at different speeds – dense objects fall faster. So a big heavy thing like a king-size duvet will fall more slowly than a small light thing like a marble. However, in a vacuum, where there is no air to create resistance, all objects fall at the same speed.)

If the Leaning Tower demonstration really happened, it was probably in 1591. Which was otherwise a bad year: Galileo's dad died, leaving him with the responsibility of paying for things like the dowry for his sister's wedding and, what was worse, his contract at Pisa University came to an end. Since he'd irritated so many people, it wasn't renewed. He was out of a job.

Lock up your daughters

But not for long. Guidobaldo found him another professorship, at Padua University this time, with a reasonable salary. So Galileo moved there and stayed with a rich friend called Gianvincenzo Pinelli. This was very handy because Gianvincenzo had a great science library and was matey with some of the most powerful people in Padua. Galileo turned out to be a popular lecturer, teaching mathematics, astronomy and mechanics.

Galileo also knew how to have a jolly good time and was often out drinking and partying like crazy. One night, after a quiet pint and several noisy ones, he and two friends fell asleep in a hotel room with an opening in the wall that led to a spooky, cold, damp cave. His two friends became ill and died and Galileo never fully recovered, suffering from rheumatism and various other aches and pains for the rest of his life. All a bit mysterious really...

After a while, Galileo moved out to a rented house, where he built something which showed just how useful his new way of doing science was – it was an instrument which could be used to aim cannon, work out square roots, calculate the amount of gunpowder needed for different sorts of cannonball and just about everything else but make tea. He called it the military compass, and the military – who had bags of money as ever – loved it.

31

He sold lots of them and, always on the look out for powerful friends, dedicated the instruction manual that went with it to an ex-pupil of his, Don Cosimo de Medici.

When Galileo was 35, he settled down with a woman called Maria Gamba, and they had three kids together. The fact that they weren't married didn't make much difference to them, but it did to their two daughters. Because they'd been born to an unmarried couple, they were – rather weirdly – considered unmarriageable themselves. Galileo sent them to a convent where they had hardly any food and worked hard for the rest of their lives – whether they liked it or not. As if that wasn't bad enough, the convent was *dead* creepy; the bones in the churchyard it contained were even supposed to rattle when one of the nuns was about to pop her clogs.

One of Galileo's daughters, Virginia, was happy at the convent and she and Galileo remained extremely fond of each other for the rest of their lives, exchanging many letters (sadly all Galileo's are lost). The other daughter, Livia, has been accused of being bad-tempered. But then, wouldn't you be?

The secret solar system

In 1543, before Galileo was born, a Polish scientist called Nicholas Copernicus had published a book suggesting the Earth went round the Sun. Aristotle, and most other people, had always assumed the Sun went round the Earth, and the Bible implied that too. But Galileo thought Copernicus was right and, in 1597, he wrote to a German scientist called Johannes Kepler about it.

Meanwhile, he had improved his theory of falling objects until he'd come up with a brilliantly simple law of fall.

He was developing this law further when something amazing happened; a star about two thousand million miles away exploded, increasing in brightness 100 million times. (Actually, the explosion took place in about 2,500 BC, but the light took until the Renaissance to reach Earth.)

Now this sort of thing would have upset Aristotle very much indeed, since it was *not* how stars were supposed to behave. They were supposed to be made of stuff that never changed, and do nothing much other than glow prettily and go round in circles. According to Aristotle, the only part of the Universe where things changed was within the orbit of the Moon, so the star would have to be there, not further away.

The Renaissance Review
BIG STAR PUNCH-UP

As everyone who has looked at the sky lately can't help spotting, a new star has appeared, and it's causing as much upset on Earth as in space.

The Aristotelians' claims that the star must be within the orbit of the Moon have been contradicted by Galileo, whose calculations show that it can't be: if it were, it would be seen in different parts of the sky depending on where it was observed from.

The Aristotelians aren't impressed. A spokesmen said today, 'Why is he bothering to make observations of something that is clearly explained in Aristotle's books anyway?'

IF THE NEW STAR EXISTED IN THE EARTH'S ATMOSPHERE...

FROM ENGLAND THE NEW STAR WOULD BE SEEN BELOW THE OLD STAR

NICE, RELIABLE OLD STAR

NEW STAR

FROM ITALY THE NEW STAR WOULD BE SEEN ABOVE THE OLD STAR

NOT TO SCALE

This sort of debate made Galileo quite famous and, oddly enough, this meant he was often asked to cast horoscopes for people, that being the sort of thing famous brainy people were expected to do in those days, rather than appearing on chat shows. And they were just as accurate then as they are today: for instance, in 1609 Galileo predicted a long and happy life for Ferdinand I de Medici, Grand Duke of Tuscany. Twenty-two days later...

Though a bit irritating for all concerned, this was also very handy. Ferdinand's death meant that Cosimo – Galileo's ex-pupil – became His Serene Highness Grand Duke Cosimo the Second. *Ideal* for Galileo, who wanted a nice cushy court job. Cosimo was Galileo's kind of guy – powerful *and* a member of a family that was very keen on the cosmos (so his name was nice and appropriate). Cosimo's grandad even identified himself with Jupiter.

Then something happened that changed Galileo from a fairly famous scientist with a few good ideas about astronomy (and an amazing theory of motion) into a really famous bloke who discovered a whole new Universe. He heard that someone had invented a tube with some glass at each end which enabled distant objects to be seen more clearly. Armed with this vague description and his gigantic brain, Galileo built his own, much better, version.

Telescopes were big news – everyone wanted one. To most people, they were just pricey toys, but to Galileo they were tools. In 1609 he pointed his home-made telescope at the night sky, and discovered:

MOUNTAINS ON THE MOON

MILLIONS OF STARS NO ONE HAD SEEN BEFORE

FOUR MOONS OF JUPITER

A PLANET THAT CHANGED SHAPE

VENUS

STILL VENUS BUT IN ANOTHER PHASE

A PLANET WITH ...ER... EARS ...OR SOMETHING

ACTUALLY IT WAS THE RINGS OF SATURN

> # SECRETS OF SCIENCE
> As the first astronomer in human history who used more than just his eyes, Galileo opened the door to observations of objects in space that would otherwise have remained hidden from humanity for ever – or at least until someone else had had a look.

Galileo quickly wrote and published a book called *The Starry Messenger* and everyone went wild with excitement. He didn't mention Saturn's ear-like extra bits, but sent his discovery to fellow astronomers, including Kepler, in the form of an anagram of 'I observed the highest planet to be triple-bodied'.

But none of the astronomers got it. This was just as well because Saturn isn't triple-bodied at all, it's just got rings round it.

All these discoveries made Galileo certain that Aristotle was wrong about his theory that everything in the Universe goes round the Earth. He could see that the moons of Jupiter didn't, for a start, and the changing size and shape of Venus only made sense if it was travelling around the Sun.

Apart from discovering a lot of new bits of the Universe in about ten minutes, Galileo's discoveries were a brilliant bargaining chip: he dedicated *The Starry Messenger* to Cosimo II, droning on endlessly about how wonderful Cosimo Medici was and calling the moons he'd found 'The Medicean Stars'. This licky behaviour did the trick and Cosimo appointed Galileo 'Chief Mathematician of the University of Pisa and Philosopher and Mathematician to the Grand Duke' (and if you think that's a long title, wait and see the sort Galileo really liked).

Jobsearch

Position: Chief Mathematician of the University of Pisa and Philosopher and Mathematician to the Grand Duke

Salary: high

Starting date: October 1610

Main duties: none whatsoever

Would suit: candidates born in Pisa, aged 46 and called Galileo

~

His Serene Highness Grand Duke Cosimo the Second is an equal opportunities employer

---

So Galileo was doing brilliantly well, but his success, his cleverness and, to be honest, his insulting and superior treatment of anyone who disagreed with him, made a group of his fellow scientists angry and envious and bent on revenge (he called them The Pigeon League because their leader's name was Mr Doves). In 1611 he went to Rome where he was elected to the world's first scientific society. It was called The Academy of the Lynx-eyed, since lynxes were famous for their amazing eyesight.

But, meanwhile…

Who are moons for?

In 1611, a German astronomer called Christopher Scheiner noticed some dark spots on the Sun and suggested they were little stars. Galileo disagreed and published some letters claiming that the spots were on the solar surface. And, as well as a certain amount of moaning about his health, he also mentioned that the Earth went round the Sun. Oh dear.

Galileo's enemies pounced. He was far too clever to defeat by disproving his theories (many of them had tried and he'd wiped the floor with them), so they criticized him on religious grounds instead. A sermon was preached, condemning Galileo as anti-religious.

Now Galileo was a religious bloke, it's just he thought that what the Bible had to say about science was rubbish.

But criticizing the Bible was dangerous – people had been burnt alive for less. Galileo didn't criticize the Bible, but he did criticize Aristotle. Yet the Church had adopted Aristotle's science, more or less, so Galileo's enemies only had to point this out and Galileo was in big trouble. He was drawn into all sorts of debates, in which he found himself having to prove that his scientific beliefs were consistent with the Bible. Given that the Bible says things like 'Thou fixed the Earth upon its foundations, not to be moved for ever,' this was a bit tricky.

Galileo was brilliantly skilled at argument and did come up with ways round whatever the Bible said, but it was a losing battle – for one thing the people who wrote the Bible almost certainly *did* think the Earth was stationary (if they thought about it at all), and for another the Catholics had an official rule that it was sinful to analyse the Bible. And anyway, word-chopping was not what Galileo wanted to be doing even though he was brilliant at it. He wanted to be a proper scientist and find out what was true and what wasn't, unlike everyone else who just tried to argue awkward discoveries out of existence. Some priests refused to even look through a telescope to see what was out there, having convinced themselves there was nothing to see. Some argued that the moons of Jupiter couldn't exist because, being invisible  to the naked eye, they could be of no possible benefit to humanity, so God wouldn't have wasted his time inventing them. They also said the mountains on the Moon didn't prove that Aristotle was wrong when he said the Moon had a smooth surface – because there might be a perfectly smooth invisible layer covering the whole Moon, mountains and all. Galileo replied:

... INDEED. WITH MASSIVE INVISIBLE MOUNTAINS ON IT.

Galileo didn't think the Bible was the right book to read if you wanted to find out about the world, and nor were Aristotle's. The book he preferred was a bit bigger: he said the truth was 'written in this grand book – the Universe – which stands continually open to our gaze, but it cannot be understood unless one learns first to comprehend the language and interpret the characters in which it is written. It is written in the language of mathematics.'

SECRETS OF SCIENCE

Galileo's insight that maths can be used to describe the world – as his law of fall and his pendulum law do – is something which allowed him and other scientists ever since not only to describe the things that happen in the Universe but to predict and control them too.

In 1615, Galileo decided to take the question to the top, to the Pope in Rome. Which was a bad move. The Pope – Paul V – was not interested in science and set up a committee to decide whether Galileo's views contradicted the Bible (never mind whether they were right). The committee decided they did and Galileo got a proper telling-off. He was also told that, unless he renounced his theory, he would be forbidden to discuss the idea of a moving Earth again. Galileo wisely, if rather unusually, did as he was told, so he was *not* forbidden. But Galileo's enemies were everywhere and a report was written stating that Galileo *had* been forbidden to discuss the idea. Very sneaky. But Galileo was sneakier. He got a signed statement to say he had *not* been forbidden. Just in case he ever needed it.

Sixteen years later, he did.

Difficult days

Now, the sensible thing for Galileo to have done would have been to keep quiet on astronomical matters and concentrate on a nice spot of motion or something. But the very next year, while he was in Rome again, he was busy writing and talking loudly in defence of Copernicus.

Again, when three comets appeared and a religious astronomer called Orazio Grassi claimed they circled the Earth within the Moon's orbit, it would have been best for Galileo to keep quiet. But…

THAT'S RUBBISH. AND BY THE WAY, THE EARTH MOVES.

Galileo might have felt safe because there was a new pope in Rome by then, Urban VIII. Urban was quite keen on a bit of science and actually liked one of Galileo's books so much he had it read to him at meals. Galileo went to Rome to see him and they got on fine, playing with a microscope Galileo built for Urban. Galileo hoped he would give him permission to say what he liked, but there was a small problem: Urban was sure the Earth was the centre of the solar system. However, he and Galileo agreed that it would be a good plan for Galileo to write a book explaining both the Sun-centred theory and the Earth-centred one, partly to show the critics of the Church that it did not stifle debate. But Galileo was *not* to conclude that the Sun-centred view was right.

Which Universe?

For the next six years, Galileo worked away at his book, one of the greatest ever written. Its rather snappy title was: *Dialogue of Galileo Galilei, Lyncean, Special Mathematician of the University of Pisa and Philosopher and Chief Mathematician of the Most Serene Grand Duke of Tuscany. Where, in the Meetings of Four Days, there is Discussion Concerning the Two Chief Systems of the World, Ptolemaic and Copernican, Propounding Inconclusively the Philosophical and Physical Reasons as Much for One Side as for the Other.*

Once you've made it through the title, (which is normally shortened to *Two World Systems*) it's a great book. It's written as a sort of play with three characters. One thinks the Earth goes round the Sun, one thinks the Sun goes around the Earth and the other is supposed to be neutral. Sadly, though, its main point – that the tides prove that the Earth moves – is wrong. The tides are caused by the gravity of the Sun and the Moon, but the law of gravity hadn't been discovered yet. The best evidence in the book for the motion of the Earth is that the planets change in size in the sky – which is not what you'd expect if they went round the Earth.

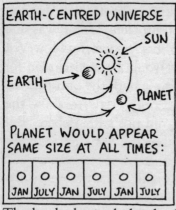

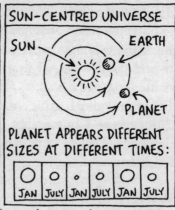

The book also includes the first relativity theory. Galileo shows that objects in the hold of a ship are unaffected by the smooth motion of the ship.

Galileo might have got his book written more quickly if his brother hadn't sent his massive family to live with him just then, saying they would be '… an amusement for you'.

The book was good news for the history of science, but it was bad news for Galileo. Very bad news indeed.

> ## ✠ Urban's Secret Pope Notes ✠
>
> I was really getting into this new book of Galileo's until Eric told me that the dumb character in it is supposed to be me! And it's dead obvious that Galileo hasn't Propounded Inconclusively the Philosophical and Physical Reasons as Much for One Side as for the Other like it says on the cover! He's proved conclusively that the Earth goes round the Sun! After I told him repeatedly it doesn't!

The book was banned and Galileo was summoned to Rome, to be tried before the scary Inquisition. In 1633 he made the long journey. He was 69 – by that age, most people in those days were dead. Galileo soon wished he was too…

Ssh! Secret scientist

Galileo had no chance. Death, imprisonment and torture were all on the cards (though probably not in that order) and the Pope was really very cross indeed – one commentator said he 'exploded'. It was lucky Galileo had that document described on page 42 saying he'd never been forbidden to consider that the Earth moved. Nevertheless he was forced to make a statement saying that the Earth absolutely definitely didn't move a centimetre in any direction whatsoever, forbidden to write anything further and sentenced to imprisonment –

for life. Blimey. So much for the Church not stifling scientific debate, eh?

Luckily Galileo still had friends as well as enemies and he was eventually allowed to serve his life sentence at home, near his daughters' convent outside Florence. He spent the rest of his life there, under house arrest, and headed letters that he wrote 'From my prison'. But he was allowed to visit his daughters, and he even managed to entertain a few visitors and talk science with them. Very quietly.

And then in 1638...

The Renaissance Review

DOUBLE DUTCH SCIENCE SURPRISE

Disgraced scientist Galileo has done it again. His latest book features not just one but two amazing new sciences. Though under house arrest and under strict instructions to stop being so scientific, Galileo wrote the book on the quiet and smuggled it out to Holland to be published.

Like his previous book, *Discourses and Mathematical Demonstrations Concerning Two New Sciences* makes science fun. Once again, it's in the form of technical chat between three blokes, one of whom is a little bit on the dumb side.

The two sciences deal with objects in motion and the strength of materials and the book is stuffed full of fascinating facts, dramatic discoveries and exciting experiments. How much does the air weigh? How fast do sound and light travel? Is everything made of atoms? Read Galileo's latest blockbuster and find out. (Unless you live in Italy, of course.)

Galileo's favourite daughter died in 1633 and, by the time *Two New Sciences* was published, he was blind but still he kept working. One of the last things he did was to invent the basis of a pendulum clock, which he got his son to draw for him. He steered well clear of the solar system, but *Two World Systems*, though banned for almost two centuries by the Church, did its work and gradually the sun-centred theory became accepted by most scientists.

GALILEO GALILEI
THAT WAS YOUR LIFE
Revolutionized:
astronomy and physics

TOP DISCOVERIES:
- law of motion
- pendulum law
- law of fall
- moons of Jupiter
- structure of solar system

NON-SCIENTIFIC INTEREST:
boozing

Though never one for undue modesty (or any at all really), Galileo, in *Two New Sciences*, said, 'There have been opened up to this vast and most excellent science ... ways and means by which other minds more acute than mine will explore its remote corners...'

One of the greatest such minds was born in 1642, the year of Galileo's death...

ISAAC NEWTON AND HIS UNIVERSAL ATTRACTION

Isaac Newton was one of the greatest scientists who ever lived, but he wasn't all that keen on science – in fact, sometimes it really got on his nerves. It's practically unheard of for a dead famous scientist – or any scientist at all – to feel like that. Look at Galileo; he loved science so much, he was willing to risk almost everything for it. And the rest of the scientists in this book are the same, more or less. But not Isaac.

Isaac was born on a farm in Woolsthorpe, Lincolnshire, on the cold Christmas Day of 1642. He was tiny, weak and not really expected to live. This depressing start was closely followed by an equally miserable childhood, partly because he was so brainy he found it difficult to relate to people, but mostly because his mum abandoned him. Because Isaac's dad had died before he was born, and because he was an only child, he and his mum, Hannah, were very close until he was three, when Hannah married a rich, much older bloke, and moved in with him, leaving Isaac to be looked after by her parents.

Eight years later, Hannah's husband died and she returned, but she brought three new children with her, whom Isaac didn't like. Perhaps it was just as well that a year later he started to go to a school 10 km away. The distance meant that during the week he lodged with the local apothecary, Mr Clark, who lent Isaac his science books, whispered the secrets of the Apothecaries Guild, and let Isaac mix medicines. For instance:

It was just as well Isaac learnt a bit of science from Mr Clark (even if it was disgusting and completely useless) because he didn't learn any at school. There, it was mainly Latin, Greek and scripture (Bible studies). Isaac really liked the scripture.

Isaac also really liked books. He found a great one called *The Mysteries of Nature and Art* and followed its instructions to make clocks, water wheels and even UFOs.

Isaac's mum didn't think much of science and took him away from school for a while to get him to help on the farm. Fortunately he was rubbish and did more harm than good and she soon let him go back again, where he got ready to go to Cambridge University.

By this stage, Isaac's mum was fairly well-off, what with her rich old hubby dying and Isaac not being there to ruin the farm. So she could have easily paid for him to have a nice easy time at university. But she didn't, and he was taken on as a subsizar instead. It wasn't a fun job. Subsizars were students who worked their way through university by doing things like cleaning rooms, emptying chamber pots and other character-building tasks. In Isaac's case, the sort of character they built was grumpy and suspicious.

Don't try this at home

In 1663, at the age of 21, Isaac suddenly began to question the scientific theories about the Universe that were knocking about just then, partly because he was a genius but also because he didn't think the theories were godly enough. One that he did rather like was the theory that everything was made of atoms, perhaps because he thought pushing atoms about would give God a job to do (a rather boring and time-consuming one if you ask me).

So Isaac, still at university, was soon involved in his own scientific research – he bought a prism and used it to make rainbow patterns on his walls. Like most people, he thought the colours were lovely (especially crimson), but unlike them he really wanted to understand exactly how they worked. He did other experiments with light too – like poking a little knife behind his eye and staring at the Sun for a long time, just to see what would happen. Surprisingly enough, he didn't blind himself.

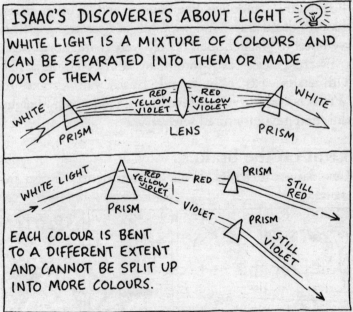

ISAAC'S DISCOVERIES ABOUT LIGHT

WHITE LIGHT IS A MIXTURE OF COLOURS AND CAN BE SEPARATED INTO THEM OR MADE OUT OF THEM.

EACH COLOUR IS BENT TO A DIFFERENT EXTENT AND CANNOT BE SPLIT UP INTO MORE COLOURS.

In 1664, Isaac suddenly got into maths in a big way and soon he knew as much as anyone. So he was all set to be a top scientist – so long as he was bright enough to pass his exams he could stay on at Cambridge which, despite the chamber pots, was just the place for him.

PASS HIS EXAMS?

Yes. Like other top scientists, Isaac preferred to work on his own, and wasn't too keen on the regular lectures, so it was by no means sure he would pass. He did though, just. However, no sooner had his future at Cambridge been assured than he had to leave it. Because of fleas.

In 1665, Cambridge, like London and all other cities, was full of rats. The rats were full of fleas and the fleas were full of plague. Soon people were dying horribly all over the place – at a rate of up to 7,000 a day. The University was closed and Isaac went home to Woolsthorpe where he stayed for 18 months. What he did there revolutionized science…

Fruit on the brain

One day – so it's said – Isaac was sitting in the orchard when…

SPLOT!

…which made him think about gravity. It's not clear quite what he thought, but here are some ideas:

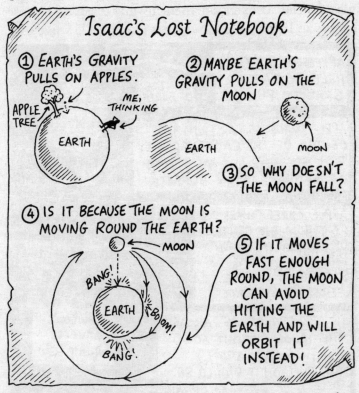

Isaac's Lost Notebook

① EARTH'S GRAVITY PULLS ON APPLES.

APPLE TREE

ME, THINKING

EARTH

② MAYBE EARTH'S GRAVITY PULLS ON THE MOON

EARTH

MOON

③ SO WHY DOESN'T THE MOON FALL?

④ IS IT BECAUSE THE MOON IS MOVING ROUND THE EARTH?

MOON

BANG!

EARTH

BOOM!

BANG!

⑤ IF IT MOVES FAST ENOUGH ROUND, THE MOON CAN AVOID HITTING THE EARTH AND WILL ORBIT IT INSTEAD!

So far, Isaac's theory made sense. But there were other theories around too, like that of Descartes, who thought there was a great, invisible sea that swept the Moon round the Earth and the Earth round the Sun. It was a nice idea but there was no real evidence for it. To find out whether there was any evidence for *his* idea, Isaac did just what Galileo said a good scientist should; he applied maths to the problem to see whether his theory worked. By then, Kepler (we met him in the last chapter) had worked out the speeds and orbits of the planets. Isaac needed to work out what sort of gravity pull the Sun would need to exert on them to make sense of those speeds and orbits. He reckoned it must be a law like this:

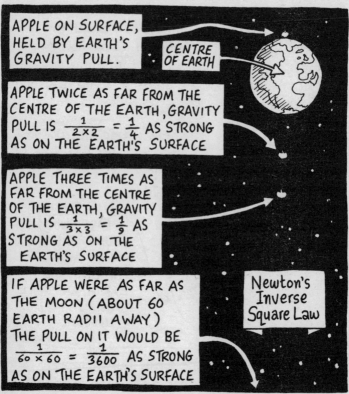

APPLE ON SURFACE, HELD BY EARTH'S GRAVITY PULL.

CENTRE OF EARTH

APPLE TWICE AS FAR FROM THE CENTRE OF THE EARTH, GRAVITY PULL IS $\frac{1}{2 \times 2} = \frac{1}{4}$ AS STRONG AS ON THE EARTH'S SURFACE

APPLE THREE TIMES AS FAR FROM THE CENTRE OF THE EARTH, GRAVITY PULL IS $\frac{1}{3 \times 3} = \frac{1}{9}$ AS STRONG AS ON THE EARTH'S SURFACE

IF APPLE WERE AS FAR AS THE MOON (ABOUT 60 EARTH RADII AWAY) THE PULL ON IT WOULD BE $\frac{1}{60 \times 60} = \frac{1}{3600}$ AS STRONG AS ON THE EARTH'S SURFACE

Newton's Inverse Square Law

The stronger the pull of gravity on the Moon, the faster it must move sideways to avoid falling to the Earth. Since the Moon's speed was known, Isaac could check whether the pull of gravity that the inverse square law predicted was of the strength required to explain the Moon's speed. But Isaac's equations didn't predict *quite* the right answer. How very annoying.

Secret science

Galileo couldn't take his 'apply maths to physics' approach very far because there was so little maths on offer at the time – just geometry and arithmetic. Isaac had something much better. Before leaving Cambridge, he'd started to develop what's now called calculus. It's a way of tracking moving objects and other changing things. Without it, it's only possible to deal with things that speed up or slow down or orbit each other in an inaccurate, fiddly and long-winded way – as Galileo had to.

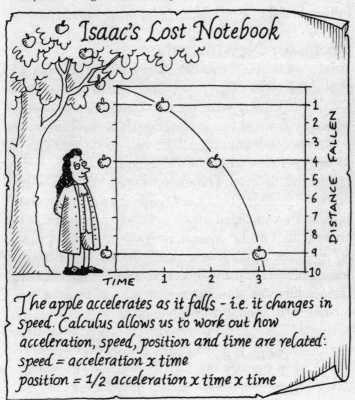

Isaac's Lost Notebook

The apple accelerates as it falls - i.e. it changes in speed. Calculus allows us to work out how acceleration, speed, position and time are related:

speed = acceleration x time

position = 1/2 acceleration x time x time

SECRETS OF SCIENCE

Calculus is the main mathematical tool scientists use to test their theories. It's applied to everything from designing cars to working out where the Universe came from.

If you'd invented a key to unlock the secrets of the Universe, wouldn't you shout about it? Isaac didn't – for years he told no one and never allowed his calculus to be fully published. Which led to a lot of arguments later on.

Professor Newton

After a while, the plague faded away, helped in London by the dead famous Great Fire (which was otherwise rather a nuisance). Isaac went back to Cambridge University, where he managed to get a fellowship which meant he could stay indefinitely. All he had to do was give 20 lectures per year, which he did – though often he had no one to give them to. The students wouldn't be examined on them, so they didn't need to go. It's a pity they didn't because they included Isaac's world-changing discoveries about light. On the other hand, none of the people who *did* go to the lectures were at all thrilled, so maybe they were a little bit on the incomprehensible side. Anyway, Isaac sometimes just lectured to an empty room for a quarter of an hour, before going off to...

DO MORE SCIENCE, I SUPPOSE

Well, no, actually. For a while, Isaac had a relatively wild and studenty time...

Isaac was matey with Professor Isaac Barrow, a top maths bloke who soon recognized how brilliant Isaac was. When Barrow resigned his professorship in 1669 to go for a new job in London, he recommended Isaac as his replacement. So, aged 26, Isaac became a proper professional professor.

Secrets and mysteries

So now Isaac had plenty of time to continue working out the Universe using his dead secret maths. But in fact he spent a lot of it doing other things. Weird things.

Isaac's Lost Notebook
Things to do: 1669

• *Work out the future history of the world from the Bible.*

• *Find a way to change lead into gold.*

• *Find a way of living for ever.*

Why was Isaac so keen on all this? For one thing, it seems that he thought that in the good old days there had been geniuses who knew everything.

Er ... no, not you. Sorry, gents. The identities of the geniuses had been lost but their amazing knowledge was legendary.

Isaac was determined to unearth these lost secrets again.

Another thing is that Isaac really, really, believed in God. But he also really, really, believed in science. This soon led him to see, just as Galileo had, that the Bible couldn't possibly be right. For instance, the accepted religious view at the time was that though there was only one God, there were also Jesus and the Holy Sprit – all equal and the same in some mysterious way. Isaac thought this was rubbish and thought the usual explanation that relied on faith, i.e. believing without reason or evidence, was pathetic as a basis of Christianity. There was no way Isaac could reject the Bible entirely, since he felt deeply that it was based on fact (as did most people in those days). He just had to make things fit.

To suss out the Universe, Isaac used three approaches: mathematical physics, analysis of the Bible and alchemy (a cross between magic and chemistry). These tools took Isaac's work in very weird directions. For instance, he thought that the measurements of an ancient temple, as given in the Bible, held the secrets of the past and future and he spent years trying to decode them.

Two of his approaches led him nowhere and the other led him to make more scientific progress than anyone in history. Guess which...

So in some ways Isaac was very old-fashioned while in others, in particular in his use of maths to solve physics problems, he was very modern. Another thing that was very modern about him was his determination to avoid 'hypotheses', by which he meant inventing theories that relied on things there could be no evidence for – like Descartes's invisible sea.

How to be a genius

It's hard to imagine how Isaac managed to come up with his amazing discoveries. He reckoned the secret was simple: 'By always thinking unto them. I keep the subject constantly before me and wait till the first dawnings open little by little into the full light.' The only thing is, concentrating that hard did make him a teeny bit absent-minded. He once started up a hill leading a horse by its bridle and got to the top to find only the bridle was still with him. Once he was discovered in his kitchen, boiling his watch with an egg in his hand. Another time, when he had a friend round for dinner, he not only forgot to order any food for him, he also forgot he was there. Happily he also forgot to eat his own dinner when it arrived so the friend ate that instead. When Isaac saw the empty plates he said 'Dear me, I thought I had not dined, but I see I have.'

A club for science

Isaac wasn't just a mathematical genius. He was also an incredibly skilled craftsman and one of the things he made was a telescope. Galileo had been excellent at making telescopes, but his were a bit unsatisfactory because they were full of rainbow colours. Isaac decided that his experiments on light proved that this was unavoidable; any lens must make rainbows.

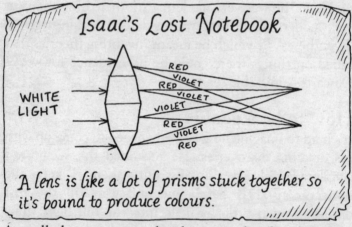

Isaac's Lost Notebook

WHITE LIGHT

RED
VIOLET
RED
VIOLET
VIOLET
RED
VIOLET
RED

A lens is like a lot of prisms stuck together so it's bound to produce colours.

Actually he was wrong, but he went ahead and made a new sort of telescope, one with a mirror instead of a lens. This had been tried before but Isaac actually made it work. He even made the tools he built it with. It was a wonderful device and Isaac Barrow asked Isaac if he could show it to his mates at the Royal Society, a scientific club that had recently been set up by the king, and which was packed with famous people.

It also had some very odd lectures, including one about werewolves...

The Royal Society loved Isaac's telescope and, when he made them one, they invited him to join. He was very pleased and sent them a paper containing his discoveries about light and colour. Most of the Royal Society loved it, but not Robert Hooke. He was a top scientist and a very jealous man too.

Despite Galileo, the scientific approach still hadn't entirely got off the ground, so no one actually bothered to do an experiment to check whether Isaac's paper was right or not until they'd argued about it for a few months. When they finally did, it showed that Isaac was, of course, right.

But by this time, Isaac was thoroughly cheesed off; he hated arguments (the complete opposite to Galileo who loved a good shouting match). So, having answered all the criticisms of his paper brilliantly, he stamped off to Cambridge to do some alchemy. He'd gone right off science in general and the Royal Society in particular. He said:

> *I see I have made myself a slave to philosophy [physics] … I will resolutely bid adieu to it eternally, excepting what I do for my private satisfaction … for I see a man must either resolve to put out nothing new, or to become a slave to defend it.*

At the same meeting where Isaac's telescope was shown off, in 1672, there was an announcement of a new measurement of the size of the Earth. Isaac, inexplicably, just took no notice, though he must have realized that it might mean his prediction of the Moon's orbit on the basis of his law of gravity was right after all. Three years later, the announcement was published in the Society's journal. Still Isaac did nothing. Then, in 1682, Isaac was at the Royal Society when there was a discussion of Picard's measurement of the Earth. This time, he *did* try his sums again and found that his 17-year-old theory gave the known speed for the Moon's orbit once the correct value for the Earth's diameter was used. It was a key moment in the history of science; a simple mathematical law had been proved to explain the movements of the planets – movements that people, including Aristotle and Galileo, had tried to explain for thousands of years.

Isaac kept quiet about it.

Left to himself, Isaac might well not have done any more science, nor published what he had achieved. For him, alone of all great scientists, it really seems that he simply didn't think science was all that important. For brief periods of his life he would feel inspired to do a bit and he'd push mankind's understanding of the Universe another step forward. But then he'd turn to alchemy or the Bible or something else instead, in the hope that they would reveal other secrets of the Universe. It's impossible to imagine what he'd have achieved if he'd made science his life's work. It also seems incredible that he couldn't see the difference between the amazing success of the science he did and the complete failure of his other research.

Keep watching the skies

Remember how in 1618 three comets appeared and changed Galileo's life? Something similar happened to Isaac in 1680. A comet appeared and a scientist called Edmund Halley started to study it. Everyone became fascinated by the way it and the planets moved; they knew their orbits were elliptical, but people like dead famous architect Christopher Wren, as well as Robert Hooke and many others, wanted to know why this was. Some thought that might be because it obeyed an inverse square law (see page 54), but it was just a guess.

Robert Hooke said he could show that the inverse square law made the planets move in ellipses and Christopher Wren offered him and Edmund Halley a nice pricey book as a prize if they could prove it. But they couldn't – and nor, it seemed, could anyone else. In August 1684, Edmund went off to see slightly famous Isaac in Cambridge in case he could help. Isaac told him he'd done it ages ago.

A few months later, Isaac sent Edmund Halley the proof – and a lot more besides. It was enough to convince Edmund that Isaac was an utter utter genius, so for the next few months he coaxed and pestered and flattered the grumpy Isaac into writing a book about motion. After a while Isaac got into it. Really into it. After years of being bored with science, he was suddenly so keen on it that he more or less gave up food and sleeping and would often wander vaguely round Cambridge when he was supposed to be going shopping and then leg it wildly back home again to write down a new discovery without even sitting down.

The result was a book as important as Galileo's, but with a much shorter title. It was called *The Mathematical Principles of Natural Philosophy*. Nowadays, it's normally known by the first word of its Latin title: the *Principia*.

A little light reading

Unlike Galileo, Isaac had no desire whatsoever to write so that people could understand him easily – they'd only pester him with daft questions. So he wrote his book in Latin and made it very complicated. Also, though he used his secret calculus to work out the results, he used a very old-fashioned geometrical approach, not unlike

Galileo's, to explain them. He did, however, helpfully provide a little reading list for people who wanted to understand the *Principia*:

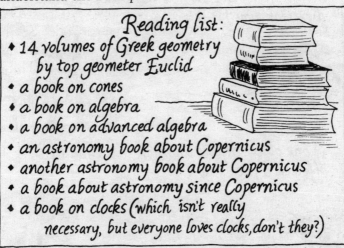

Reading list:
* 14 volumes of Greek geometry by top geometer Euclid
* a book on cones
* a book on algebra
* a book on advanced algebra
* an astronomy book about Copernicus
* another astronomy book about Copernicus
* a book about astronomy since Copernicus
* a book on clocks (which isn't really necessary, but everyone loves clocks, don't they?)

So the *Principia* was a bit of a tricky read. And it was constructed so that you couldn't just dip in at the juicy bits. You had to read it from beginning to end to have even a slim chance of understanding it.

What the *Principia* said was:

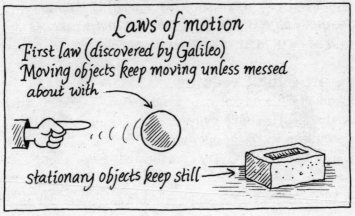

Laws of motion
First law (discovered by Galileo)
Moving objects keep moving unless messed about with

stationary objects keep still

Second law
If you hit an object, its new speed and direction depend on how hard and in what direction you hit it.

WHACK!

Third law
If one object affects another, it is equally affected by it.

BOINK!

Law of gravity
Every object in the Universe attracts every other object, and the gravity pull between two objects (e.g. apple and the Earth) is stronger if the objects are more massive, and weaker if they are farther apart.

Not many people understood the *Principia* but it made Isaac dead famous. In it, after a lot of rather long-winded bits, Isaac says dramatically, 'I now demonstrate the frame of the system of the world' – *and he does*. He gives a working mathematical model of the whole solar system that not only explains it all but allows its future to be predicted. As if that wasn't enough, he explained how to weigh planets...

Planets with moons hold them in place with gravity. The heavier the planet, the stronger its gravity, so the faster its moon(s) orbit to avoid spiralling in. So by measuring the speed of a moon, the mass of the planet can be calculated.

He even succeeded where Aristotle and Galileo had failed and explained the tides...

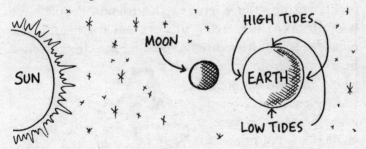

Tides are caused mainly by the Moon's gravity and partly by the Sun's gravity. When the Sun, Earth and the Moon are lined up, tides are highest.

SECRETS OF SCIENCE

Isaac's laws of gravitation and motion have been used to predict the future, work out the past and understand the present ever since. They are what got astronauts to the Moon and space probes to the planets.

A bleak winter

Isaac seems to have had very few love affairs in his life but there is some evidence that he had one or two – one with a girl called Catherine Storer when he was 17 and another with a Swiss mathematician called Nicholas Fatio de Duillier when he was about 51, soon after he'd written the *Principia*. What few letters between Isaac and Nicholas survive have had so many bits removed from them that not much is known about their relationship, and being gay would have been something Isaac had to keep secret.

In the winter of 1692-3, something strange happened to Isaac; he had some kind of mental breakdown and began writing strange letters to his friends. People have had fun ever since trying to work out the cause. One nice idea is that he spotted some time-travelling science historians from the future who'd come to admire him.

Anyway, he recovered when he found a new challenge – but not a scientific one. He was made Master of the Mint.

The Mint was where England's coins were made, and they needed a bit of looking after just then because people had taken to chopping bits off them to reuse the metal. By the time Isaac arrived on the scene, the average weight of a coin was only about half what it should be.

Isaac got into his job almost as much as he'd got into writing the *Principia*. He made sure new coins had patterned edges so you could see if they'd been chopped off. He made the Mint much more efficient and even tracked down counterfeiters personally, making quite sure they were hanged. He even bought criminal-looking clothes for 'conversing with a gang of coiners of note'.

The ocean of truth

In 1703, Isaac's old rival, Hooke, died. With Hooke and his criticisms now safely absent from the Royal Society, Isaac became interested in it again. In fact, he got himself elected as its boss. He was called its president, but he acted more like its dictator, forcing it to move to new premises, expelling people he didn't like and getting it as well-organized as the Mint. No papers about werewolves now – it all got a lot more scientific.

And so did Isaac; he pulled together all the work he'd done in optics and wrote a book called *Opticks*. And this time, possibly having softened very slightly with age, he wrote it in English. It included the work he'd done way back in 1663 (see page 51), as well as lots of new breakthroughs.

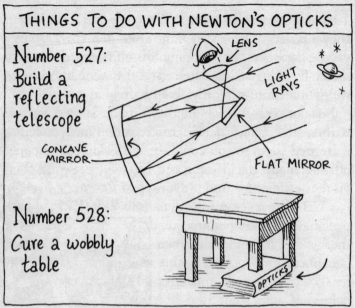

THINGS TO DO WITH NEWTON'S OPTICKS

Number 527:
Build a
reflecting
telescope

LENS

LIGHT RAYS

CONCAVE MIRROR

FLAT MIRROR

Number 528:
Cure a wobbly
table

OPTICKS

Opticks is a much more chatty book than the *Principia*, and in writing it Isaac relaxed to such an extent that he speculated about things he couldn't prove – something which, a few years before, he had refused to do. Some of these ideas took nearly two centuries to prove, and the most important ones are that light particles behave like waves, and that matter and light can change into each other. Sadly, he didn't include any details of these stunningly advanced theories.

Isaac was the greatest scientist there'd ever been and he knew it, but he knew too that science had much further to go. Not long before he died, he said he thought of himself as 'like a little boy playing on the seashore, and diverting myself in now and then finding a smoother pebble or a prettier shell than ordinary, whilst the great ocean of truth lay all undiscovered before me.'

The final problems

Maybe Isaac got friendlier as he got older – he certainly was very good to his family and friends and gave them plenty of money when they needed it. But he also got into major rows with other scientists.

One of these was Gottfried Leibniz, a German mathematician who had invented calculus independently of Isaac. After a lot of argy-bargy Isaac selected a panel of scientists to decide who invented calculus and then wrote their report himself. Guess what it said?

Then there was Flamsteed, an astronomer whose data on the Moon Isaac needed in order to prove some bits of his theories. Flamsteed was reluctant to provide it and Isaac wrote him gradually more insulting letters about it. Finally they had a big row which, according to Flamsteed, went something like this:

…and went downhill from there. Isaac called Flamsteed terrible things, including 'puppy' – presumably a shockingly bitter insult in the eighteenth century.

After he'd seen off his rivals, Isaac's last few years were fairly quiet and he died aged 84, uncomplaining about the pain of his illness and showing no fear of death. He was buried in Westminster Abbey, having been dead famous for ages by then.

And quite right too. Whether it was building the world's best telescope or coming up with the most powerful scientific theory ever, Isaac was unique in developing both the tools for the job and a stunningly effective end result. And yet he treated his science as a sideline, just one ship to explore the ocean of truth.

ISAAC NEWTON
THAT WAS YOUR LIFE
Revolutionized:
physics, mathematics and astronomy

TOP DISCOVERIES:
- calculus
- laws of motion
- law of gravitation
- laws of optics

NON-SCIENTIFIC INTERESTS:
alchemy, the Bible, crimson

MICHAEL FARADAY AND HIS ELECTRIFYING EXPERIMENTS

Michael Faraday was born in a London slum in 1791. His parents had almost no money at all, which meant there wasn't much in the way of school for him and he was never much of a mathematician. Yet he made massive breakthroughs in chemistry and physics, invented new forms of technology which started off the world's electrical industry and, alongside Galileo, was one of the greatest experimental physicists of all.

Lack of cash meant Michael had to leave school at 13 to get a job – as a messenger boy for a bookbinder called Monsieur Riebau. Being reliable, bright and hard-working meant it wasn't long before Monsieur Riebau made him an apprentice bookbinder. It might not sound a very promising start for a top scientist, but actually it turned out to be very useful – he read a lot of the books he bound and soon developed a fascination with science. He was especially interested in an article on electricity in the *Encyclopedia Britannica* and built himself various electrical gizmos.

As well as reading and bookbinding, Michael occasionally had a bit of a sing with his fellow apprentices (one of them went on to be a professional singer, and the other a comedian). It must have been rather irritating for Monsieur Riebau, though perhaps it made for a nice jolly working atmosphere.

Michael had an older brother called Tom, who would sometimes give him a bit of cash, which Michael spent on attending science lectures. He liked these so much that he not only made notes about them, he also wrote the notes up, illustrated them (he was a good artist and his visual imagination made up for his lack of mathematics when he became a scientist) and bound them. One lot of lectures were by a scientist called Humphry Davy, who was Professor of Chemistry at a scientific society called the Royal Institution. Humphry was so interesting, not to mention sexy, that his lectures were full of trendy posh women – which was a nice little earner for the Royal Institution.

The benefits of bangs

Michael loved Davy's lectures and became more and more keen on science and the idea of becoming a scientist. He sent the bound notes he made of Humphry's lectures to Humphry himself, who invited him round for a cuppa. A top scientist inviting a working-class kid for tea was stunning in those days, so Michael went along, full of excitement, but was disappointed when Humphry suggested that, scientific jobs being as rare as they were, he should stick to bookbinding.

Then, in October 1812…

Humphry was somewhat battered and, remembering Michael's keenness, asked him to help out as a temporary assistant. Michael loved the job and so impressed Davy that when one of the other assistants was sacked for fighting, he offered him a permanent job and a salary of one pound a year. Michael accepted instantly and in March 1813 he started work as a chemistry assistant.

The next few months were packed with science and Michael had a great time, despite the dangers…

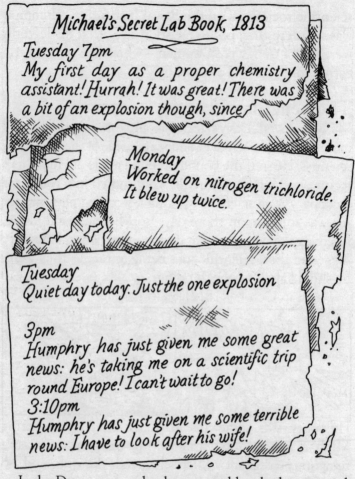

Michael's Secret Lab Book, 1813

Tuesday 7pm
My first day as a proper chemistry assistant! Hurrah! It was great! There was a bit of an explosion though, since

Monday
Worked on nitrogen trichloride. It blew up twice.

Tuesday
Quiet day today. Just the one explosion

3pm
Humphry has just given me some great news: he's taking me on a scientific trip round Europe! I can't wait to go!
3:10pm
Humphry has just given me some terrible news: I have to look after his wife!

Lady Davy was rude, bossy, snobby, bad tempered, critical and thoroughly terrifying. As if she wasn't bad enough, there was a war on with France. Luckily, in those days people thought science was so incredibly impractical that it could have no possible influence on war, so Napoleon had no objections to Michael, Humphry and the scary Lady Davy travelling through France.

Over the next 18 months…

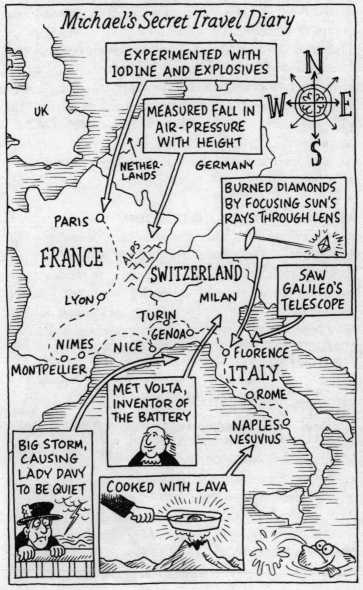

Michael didn't have many interests outside science. He did have a hobby but it wasn't anything normal like stamps or butterflies. It was chlorine, a poisonous gas in a fetching shade of greenish yellow which he managed to liquefy and to combine with carbon – both world firsts. With hobbies like that, it didn't take long before Michael became the top chemist in town, discovering and inventing things like: rustless steel (1820), benzene (1825), and glass for telescope lenses (1829). All of which success seems to have made Humphry a little bit jealous.

Michael's magnetic mission

Electricity was still a fairly new and exotic discovery – the first battery had only been invented in 1799, and all most people knew about it was that it could give them a nasty shock. Scientists thought electricity was some kind of weird fluid. This could explain most of the things it did, but not a new discovery by Hans Christian Oersted in 1820…

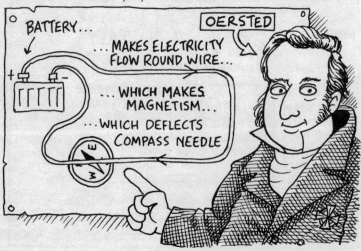

Now, this was very odd. Michael was fascinated and was soon into electricity in a big way. He stayed that way for the rest of his life, only dragging himself away from it briefly in 1821, when he married Sarah Barnard.

Michael was sure that Oersted's discovery could be reversed – that electricity could be made from magnetism. It was lucky he was patient, because it took him ten years to prove it. Along the way, he became more and more convinced that there was some fundamental link between the two things:

> ## Michael's Secret Lab Book
> I'm sure there's a basic simplicity underlying nature. I feel convinced that electricity, magnetism, gravity and other forces are all related in some way. Could they even be just different ways of looking at the same thing?

So Michael began to study the question of what magnetism actually was. Gradually, he became convinced that it was a type of force field, a bit like gravity.

Gravity, now Newton had found the mathematical law that governed it, could explain the motions of almost all objects. But Isaac knew it could not explain the way atoms interacted. It's impressive that he even considered the forces between atoms since the idea that atoms existed was not at all well-accepted. (It would take Albert Einstein to prove they were real.) Isaac even realized that the forces between atoms must be strong pushes and strong pulls, rather than just weak pulls like gravity. These forces are actually electromagnetic ones, and Michael Faraday was one of the scientists who discovered how they worked. He was the first to understand that things like magnets, electrically charged objects, wires carrying electricity, planets and apples affect one another by setting up around themselves regions of space filled – in some mysterious way – with force. Force fields.

SECRETS OF SCIENCE

The idea of force fields, which Faraday came up with, proved to be a way of explaining a great deal of the Universe. Many scientists from Einstein onwards thought – and think – that the whole Universe, even the matter it contains, is really a gigantic, enormously complicated, force field.

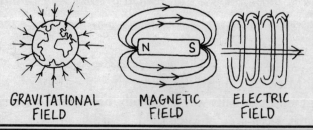

GRAVITATIONAL   MAGNETIC   ELECTRIC
FIELD   FIELD   FIELD

This is a job for...

Michael might have made much faster progress if it hadn't been for Humphry:

The assistant turned out to be a Sergeant Anderson, who was the kind of do-what-you're-told-and-don't-chat bloke the army turns out in battalions. Michael and he got on very well, working silently away for hours.

It may be that Humphry gave Michael this job deliberately to keep him busy so he wouldn't cramp his style. (He was a bit cross with him anyway, because Michael had followed up some of Humphry's ideas about electricity without mentioning him in the report he wrote.) Humphry also voted against Michael's membership of the Royal Society. On the other hand, Humphry *was* responsible for promoting Michael to director of the Laboratory of the Royal Institution in 1825.

One aspect of the work was all too familiar...

Another thing Michael had on his list of things to do just then was saving the Royal Institution from disaster. It had no money, especially after Humphry stopped lecturing in 1812 and the supply of rich, trendy women dried up a bit. Michael wasn't quite as sexy, but he was a brilliant lecturer, and he was soon attracting lots of people to his Friday evening public lectures. So Michael soon had a new hobby: education. Not bad for someone who'd had hardly any of the stuff himself.

The lectures were about everything from magnetism to 'The Condition and Ventilation of the Coal-Mine Goat'. Having been forced to become an expert on explosions, Michael included plenty in his lectures. The Royal Institution still gives public lectures, including the Christmas Lectures that Michael started in 1827.

In 1829 Humphry died, which meant Michael and Sergeant Anderson could finally stop working on the boring glass project. The next year Michael invented the electric motor.

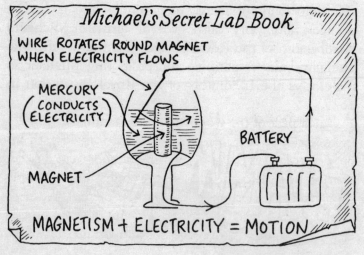

Michael's Secret Lab Book

WIRE ROTATES ROUND MAGNET WHEN ELECTRICITY FLOWS

MERCURY (CONDUCTS ELECTRICITY)

BATTERY

MAGNET

MAGNETISM + ELECTRICITY = MOTION

This could have made him rich but he wasn't really interested in money. Then in 1831 he reversed the principle of the motor and invented the electric generator or dynamo.

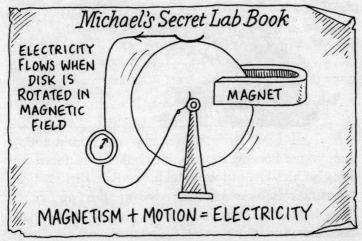

Michael's Secret Lab Book

ELECTRICITY FLOWS WHEN DISK IS ROTATED IN MAGNETIC FIELD

MAGNET

MAGNETISM + MOTION = ELECTRICITY

This was another potential money-spinner but again Michael didn't bother. What really mattered to him was that he'd done what he'd been trying to do for the last decade: make electricity from magnetism. A third opportunity for riches came along soon after when he discovered electroplating – a method of coating objects with layers of metal by means of electricity.

A simpler world?

Encouraged by his success, Michael continued with his project to prove that all natural forces were linked, starting with electricity. At the time, many people thought that there were a lot of different types of electricity but, over the next six years, Michael proved that there was really only one. An important part of his research was the measurement of the strength of electricity. These days, there are lots of instruments you can use for this. But all Michael had was his body – he used his arms, his tongue and even his eyes.

Michael loved electrical storms and would follow them round London in taxis. He could easily afford this since he had lots of jobs outside the Royal Institution, including acting as a scientific adviser in the Law Courts. He would have been rich if he hadn't handed all his extra cash to the Institution to pay for more scientific research.

By now, Michael was becoming dead famous. He received honours from the Paris Academy of Sciences and four other overseas academic establishments (even though he didn't really hold with foreigners). He and his wife went to lots of parties and met painters like Turner and writers like Dickens (even though he preferred staying at home and working). Though he had no children, he had a small pack of nephews and nieces whom he used to amuse by blowing things up from time to time.

Gradually, Michael built up his theory that all forces are linked, discovering that, whatever electrical thing he stuck in his eye and however much it hurt, the electricity itself was the same. He also found that electricity, like magnetism, generated a force field.

A real mark of Michael's genius was something which Newton and Einstein shared (but Aristotle didn't); when he couldn't explain something properly, he was content to leave it mysterious rather than come up with some half-baked theory which he was unable to prove. In this case, what he left out was the question as to what the force fields really were. Today, thanks to Einstein, we know that they are distortions in the fabric of space and time.

The decline

In 1839, everything was going brilliantly for Michael: he'd been the Royal Institution's Professor of Chemistry since 1834, he was a dead famous scientist, he had a great family, plenty of cash, lots of people to lecture to, and was steadily collecting evidence for his idea that all forces were linked. But that year he suffered a mysterious breakdown. Some people say it was due to mercury poisoning, but whatever it was it affected his mind. He became dizzy and unable to concentrate. It wasn't until 1844 that he was able to resume work, and from then on he spent all his time either in his laboratory, or with his family, or lecturing about science.

Michael's health wasn't his only problem. Apart from science and being married, there was one other thing Michael really liked, and that was a nice bit of religion. He belonged to an extreme sect called the Sandemanians who believed in the absolute truth of the Bible.

This seems a bit strange. Like all good scientists, Michael demanded that every statement must be supported by good evidence if it was to be accepted as true – except for every single statement in the Bible.

Anyway, the Sandemanians were so keen on Michael they elected him to be an elder of their church. But, one Sunday in 1844, so it's said, he was invited to dinner with Queen Victoria. For someone as fanatically religious as he was, Sundays were special and as an elder of his church he was expected to be there. But the invite was just too tempting so he went to dinner – and was expelled from the eldership for 16 years!

The terrors of science

In 1846, a scientist called Wheatstone was due to give a lecture to the Royal Institution but was overcome by nerves at the last minute and ran away. Michael stepped in and gave the lecture instead and then, finding there was plenty of time left over, gave an extra little talk of his own, about his Theory of Ray Vibrations, which said that light rays are waves that travel through space along lines of force. Though it's not quite correct, this idea led eventually to the discovery of radio waves, broadcasting, mobile phones and the Teletubbies. The incident also led to Royal Institution lecturers being locked up for half an hour before their talks, so they couldn't leg it.

Michael's efforts to find the underlying, unifying principle of nature continued. He was particularly keen to link electromagnetism and gravitation.

After a lot of patient fiddling about, Michael gave up. Many other scientists since have also tried to link electricity and gravitation. So far, they have all failed.

SECRETS OF SCIENCE

Since Michael's time, scientists have tried using new forms of mathematics as well as bigger and more complex experiments in their attempts to show that all forces are linked. It's now believed that there are four forces in nature: gravity, electromagnetism, the strong force that holds atoms together and the weak force that breaks particles apart. So far, scientists have managed to link only the electromagnetic and weak forces, by showing that, at high enough temperatures, they have exactly the same effects. The unification of all forces would mean the whole lot could be explained by a single set of linked equations.

Gradually, the mysterious disease that Michael had suffered from since 1839 worsened. His mind failed, filling slowly with a fog into which all his memories faded. One by one, he gave up all his responsibilities and resigned from all his jobs. His last Christmas lecture was in 1860, his last public lecture in 1862. In 1864 he resigned from the eldership of the Sandemanians and the next year he left the Royal Institution. By 1866 he could do little more than sit quietly in his chair all day, gazing into space.

Michael Faraday died in 1867, having begun one of science's greatest theoretical breakthroughs, which became known as field theory. He had also started one of its greatest practical achievements, the electrical industry. Never again could anyone believe, as Napoleon had, that science had no practical influence on the world.

MICHAEL FARADAY
THAT WAS YOUR LIFE
Revolutionized:
chemistry and physics

TOP DISCOVERIES:
- new materials
- laws of electricity
- electric motor and electric generator
- force fields

NON-SCIENTIFIC INTEREST:
religion

Michael left a lot of friends too, and one of them was Charles Darwin.

CHARLES DARWIN AND HIS MYSTERIOUS MONSTERS

Charles Darwin discovered some monsters that changed the world and, though he wanted a quiet life, he caused more debate than any other scientist.

Charles was born in Shrewsbury in 1809. His mother died when he was eight, so he was brought up by his sisters and his father Robert, who was a bit scary. Robert weighed 24 stone and became extremely shouty when roused. When he wasn't roused, however, he was great, and Charles and he got on just fine. Mostly. Robert once predicted:

> *You care for nothing but shooting, dogs, and rat-catching, and you will be a disgrace to yourself and all your family.*

Charles himself was bit of a late developer…

𝕾𝖈𝖍𝖔𝖔𝖑 𝕽𝖊𝖕𝖔𝖗𝖙	
English:	Average
Latin:	Average
Mathematics:	Average
Geography:	Average
History:	Average
French:	Average
General Comments:	

Charles is a timid boy and he's not the most exciting of pupils. The most interesting thing he does is collect beetles. Also shells.

In fact, one of his teachers said, 'The boy is entirely dull.'

I may not be a doctor, but I'm cheap

When he was 16, Charles's dad encouraged him to try curing local people who couldn't afford a proper doctor and *then* sent him to Edinburgh University to learn to be a medic. (Charles's patients might possibly have been happier – not to say healthier – if he'd done the learning bit first.)

Like Galileo, Charles wasn't impressed with medicine. He found the lectures dull, the subject boring and as for the operations he had to witness – all performed without anaesthetic – well, he just wasn't too keen, frankly.

TYPICAL! JUST WHEN I'D GOT THE EYES OUT!

90

Practically everyone in Charles's house was ill a lot of the time, plus his dad was a medical doctor and his sister loved wearing an anti-cold mask of her own invention, so he'd probably had quite enough of medicine at home. So, like Galileo once again, the lectures he went to at the university were nothing to do with medicine – in his case, they were geological ones.

He didn't quite dare tell his dad how much he hated medicine, but he did the next best thing and got his sisters to do it for him. His dad made a slight fuss but said he could be a clergyman instead if he liked. (In those days there were only a few respectable careers for gentlemen, such as medicine, the Church, the Army, the Navy, politics or law.) So, at 19, Charles went off to Cambridge University to study religion. Though he wasn't actually interested in it, at least he believed every word of the Bible, which was handy.

Charles had fun at Cambridge, hunting and shooting animals and making friends. He made two sorts of friends: 'dissipated low-minded young men', with whom he got drunk, sung and shot things; and senior scientists, with whom he discussed science. One of his best buddies was the Professor of Biology, Henslow, who made  Charles even keener on geology – he sent Charles off on a geological expedition to North Wales. While he was there, Charles also collected animals from tidal pools and tried to dissect them, much like Aristotle but a lot more messily since he wasn't too skilled at dissection.

When Charles got home, he found an exciting letter waiting for him from Henslow, who said that there was a place available for a naturalist to take part in a scientific expedition on a ship called the *Beagle*. Despite having no scientific qualifications, there being no pay on offer, and the fact that he was a bit shy, Charles really wanted to go. But he wasn't sure his dad would approve. And he was quite right. However, his dad did say, 'If you can find any man of common sense who advises you to go I will give my consent.' Luckily, Charles knew just the chap – one of his dad's favourite people.

I'LL TALK TO UNCLE JOS

Uncle Jos was Josiah Wedgwood, whose factory made the china they now rave about on the *Antiques Roadshow*. Charles went to see him, and Jos not only agreed with him, he travelled back with Charles to talk his dad into the idea. And so, with no degree or any clear idea about what he wanted to do with his life...

To boldly go...

On 27 December 1831 the voyage began, with Charles as scientific adviser. It was a bit like *Star Trek* – a long mission to exciting unknown places – with Charles as science officer instead of Mr Spock. The only differences were:

- Charles wasn't actually a scientist
- he was terribly seasick
- he didn't know how to do the Vulcan mind-meld. (Although he did have slightly pointy ears.)

Charles also had a squidgy little nose. This put Captain Robert Fitzroy off him like a shot. Fitzroy was into noses and had a particularly nice one of his own. He thought you could tell all sorts of things about a person from the shape of their nose, and when he saw Charles's he smelt trouble.

However, Charles had a brilliant time on his voyage, despite a great deal of seasickness and a few arguments with Fitzroy – mostly caused by having to share a tiny cabin with him for five years.

When the *Beagle* arrived at the Cape Verde Islands, Charles set foot in a tropical forest for the first time. And he was amazed – the huge variety of animals and plants was stunning. Charles started to collect like crazy – spiders, shells, beetles – he loved everything, even the vicious army ants, the scary vampire bats and the weird, clicking butterflies. The only thing he wasn't too keen on was being attacked in his sleep one night by a swarm of three-centimetre-long blood-sucking insects.

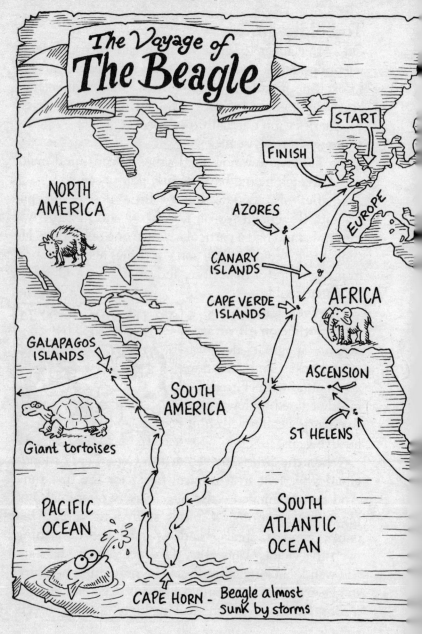

The Voyage of
The Beagle

START

FINISH

EUROPE

NORTH
AMERICA

AZORES

CANARY
ISLANDS

CAPE VERDE
ISLANDS

AFRICA

GALAPAGOS
ISLANDS

ASCENSION

SOUTH
AMERICA

ST HELENS

Giant tortoises

PACIFIC
OCEAN

SOUTH
ATLANTIC
OCEAN

CAPE HORN - Beagle almost
sunk by storms

94

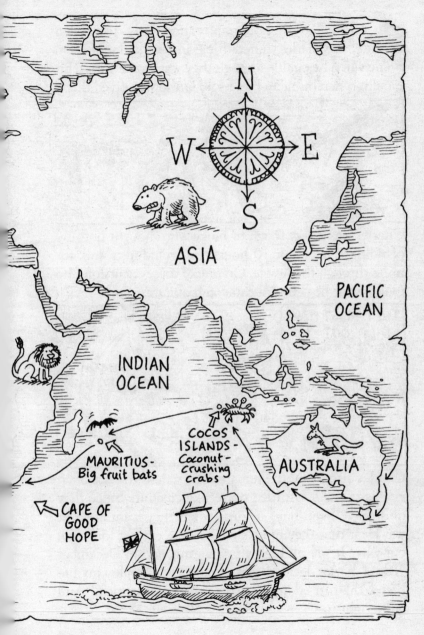

N

W E

S

ASIA

PACIFIC
OCEAN

INDIAN
OCEAN

MAURITIUS-
Big fruit bats

COCOS
ISLANDS-
Coconut-
crushing
crabs

AUSTRALIA

CAPE OF
GOOD
HOPE

In those days, photography had only just been invented so Charles stuffed things instead and sent them home when he could – though they were sometimes a bit mouldy when his mate Professor Henslow received them.

Charles was a very tough fit bloke who thought nothing of riding a horse for 10 hours. He would also walk for miles through the jungle. On one of these excursions, he found what he called 'a catacomb of monsters'...

Charles also found the remains of a rodent the size of an elephant and a fossilized horse-like creature. Since they must have been hard to miss when they were alive, it was clear that they must have become extinct long ago; but why? It was all highly fascinating, and in December 1832, Charles decided that, 'I could not employ my life better than in adding a little to natural science.' And quite right too.

In 1835 the *Beagle* landed at the Galapagos Islands, which were covered in black sand, smelled like they'd been in the oven too long and were populated by giant tortoises which Charles liked to ride about on and then eat. (Charming, eh? But they were *very* yummy.)

Charles found that each of the islands had its own variety of tortoise and finch. The finches' beaks were designed to cope with whatever lunch was on offer in each island – polite and delicate little beaks for dainty seeds, pointy pecky ones for squirmy worms, huge scary ones for heavy nuts.

All very handy, and all very odd. According to the accepted view at the time, all animal species were created by God for ever.

So God must have designed slightly different animals for each island...

...which seemed a bit strange.

The fight for life

After five years Charles was home again, in a ship bulging with samples and with a mind bursting with ideas. One idea was clear to him – despite what religion said, species *did* alter over time; the fossils he'd found, as well as the living creatures he'd seen, had made him quite convinced of that. They gradually became more adapted to their environments, like the finches' beaks. In other words, they *evolved*. But how? He needed a long think to sort it all out. A very long think indeed.

The first thing Charles did was to rent some rooms in Cambridge and sort out his samples, helped by Simms Covington, the man who played the fiddle on the *Beagle*, and a Professor Richard Owen, whom he'd met at a Geological Society dinner. Charles also started to write up his adventures.

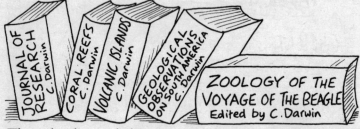

These books, and the scientific letters he'd sent home from his voyage, turned Darwin into a fairly well-known and well-respected scientist and he made two new scientific mates as a result – top geologist Charles Lyell and top botanist Joseph Hooker. This was to be very handy later. Professor Owen on the other hand... Well, let's wait and see.

Charles kept on pondering his baby theory of evolution, and one day he read a book 'for amusement' which was all about how everyone would die of starvation pretty soon. It was a nice simple theory:

Charles realized that this was just what he needed to add to his theory.

Darwin's Lost Collecting Book

Got it! This is how it works:
1. Every pair of animals produces many children and many many grandchildren – enough to cover the whole earth in a few generations if they all survived.

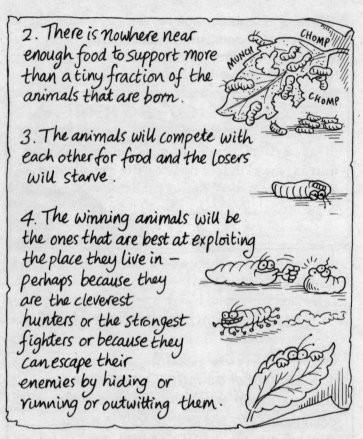

2. There is nowhere near enough food to support more than a tiny fraction of the animals that are born.

3. The animals will compete with each other for food and the losers will starve.

4. The winning animals will be the ones that are best at exploiting the place they live in — perhaps because they are the cleverest hunters or the strongest fighters or because they can escape their enemies by hiding or running or outwitting them.

Charles called this process, by which strong creatures survived and weak ones died, 'natural selection'. It was how evolution worked.

So Charles now had the basic explanation of the incredible variety of living things on earth, from jellyfish to eagles to oak trees. Each is ideally suited to the place it lives and the things it has to put up with, and those winning behaviours and bodies emerged over many generations of conflict between differently structured creatures. The conflict caused creatures with inferior bodies to die out. Suddenly, the whole natural world fell into place – without the need for God to patiently design everything.

SECRETS OF SCIENCE

After Charles, people applied the idea of evolution to all sorts of things, even computer programs; instead of working out how to write a program to do a job, programmers can just tell the computer to come up with lots of slightly different programs and let them compete to see which does the job best.

A logical love affair

Charles didn't spend all his time thinking about biology. In 1837 he reckoned it was time to get married. Maybe. Being a good scientist, he drew up a list of pros and cons:

BALANCE SHEET:
On Getting Married

PROS	CONS
Kids	Less time to study evolution
Music & chitchat	Fewer expeditions
Friend in old age	More relatives to visit

Charles concluded that, theoretically speaking, he ought to find a wife and in 1839, just after being elected a Fellow of the Royal Society, he married his cousin, Emma Wedgwood. Though a rather odd way to go about it, the marriage was successful and they had loads of kids.

Charles and Emma moved to a house in London and had a busy social life – but not for long. By the autumn of 1839, Charles found he was getting very tired. Though only 30, from then on he was never really well again – sometimes he was too ill to work for days. It's a mystery what this illness was, but on the whole people now think it was a psychological disorder.

In 1842, Charles and Emma moved to Down House, in Downe on the Downs. Every other dead famous scientist had some institution in which they did and discussed a lot of their work – like Aristotle's Lyceum, Newton's Royal Society, and Faraday's Royal Institution. Charles didn't, but he turned his house and gardens into a research centre of his own: he even filled a greenhouse with flesh-eating plants.

A bit of a nuisance

That same year Charles wrote a 35-page summary of his theory of evolution, and extended it to 230 pages in 1844. But he just showed it to a few friends and didn't publish it.

WHY NOT?

There were actually quite a few goodish reasons why Charles was so keen not to publish:

- he was very cautious by nature
- he knew it would upset religious people like his wife
- he hadn't ironed all the bugs out of it yet.

The fact that evolution contradicted the Bible didn't make Charles doubt its truth. He had decided that there was no evidence whatsoever that the Bible was true anyway. And he thought Christianity was worse than nonsense.

> *I can indeed hardly see how anyone ought to wish Christianity to be true; for if so the plain language of the text seems to show that the men who do not believe, and this would include my Father, Brother and almost all my best friends, will be everlastingly punished. And this is a damnable doctrine.*

In 1846 Charles had a little break from polishing his theory of evolution to do some work on barnacles, the nasty shelly things that stick to your bottom if you're a ship. Charles had found a weird type of South American burrowing barnacle and was soon fascinated by them. Eight years later (Charles was a terribly thorough bloke) it was back to evolution again, which he went on not publishing. As keen a collector as he'd been all his life, what Charles was collecting now was facts – facts to support his theory of evolution so that, if he ever *did* publish it, it would knock people's socks off.

Finally, in 1856, he reckoned he'd collected enough facts to convince everyone that evolution was correct, and started to write a massive book about it, which was to be about three-quarters of a million words long – more than 20 times as long as this book.

Two years later…

Wallace agreed, and they did, but no one much noticed the report anyway.

Charles now really did think he ought to get on with it. During the next 13 months he rattled off *On the Origin of Species by Natural Selection*. He didn't think it would do too well, so his publisher only printed 1,250 copies, which sold out on the day of publication. It probably helped that Hooker and Lyell both supported it and the country's top zoologist, Thomas Huxley, wrote an enthusiastic review too.

But then a lot of people got very cross…

Monkeying with the Bible

Charles had carefully avoided saying anything specific about the evolution of human beings, but it didn't take a genius to get the point; if evolution was true, it must mean humans, like all other living things, were descended from some primitive creature or other. Most people assumed this creature was a monkey though Charles and other proper scientists knew it wasn't – on the quiet, Charles thought people were descended from underwater octopus-snail kind of things. With big tails.

Lots of scientists were very critical, including Professor Richard Owen, Charles's former colleague, who wrote anonymously to the papers criticizing Charles and deliberately misquoting him. People just couldn't believe their dear old mum and dad were slightly developed monkeys. Priests went into frenzies and there was in fact a *stunning* amount of argy-bargy.

It wasn't just that Charles had overturned the idea that Adam and Eve were the remote grandad and granny of us all: he'd cast doubt on the Church's version of the Earth's history, too, by showing that it must be millions of years old, not 6,000 or so as the Bible implied.

SECRETS OF SCIENCE

Until Darwin came along, people thought of the age of the Earth and the rest of the Universe in terms of thousands of years – long time periods, but well within the grasp of the human imagination. After Darwin, people got a lot more realistic: and it rapidly became clear that the Earth was far older than anyone could imagine. It's now known the Earth is about four and a half thousand million years old, and the Universe is around thirteen thousand million years old.

Things all came to a head at a famous meeting in Oxford in 1860. Encouraged by Richard Owen, a particularly slippery bishop nicknamed Soapy Sam gave a speech rubbishing evolution and ending up asking, 'Is it through his grandfather or his grandmother that he claims descent from a monkey?' Charles, being ill at the time, wasn't there to defend himself, but his friend and fellow-scientist Thomas Huxley was. First, Huxley explained the theory in a convincing way and then he said: 'I'd rather be related to an ape than a bishop.' Which was so awfully shocking that a woman fainted.

From then on, Huxley called himself Darwin's Bulldog, with a mission to stand up for evolution. This suited Charles fine – he didn't want a lot of debate, he just wanted to be left alone with his family, his research and his writing. He wrote lots of books, mostly really thick ones stuffed full of scientific theories and lots and lots of lovely observations he'd carefully collected.

THE DESCENT OF MAN

Why are peacocks so stylish? Why are your ears like that? And who – or what - did you evolve from? All these questions and many more are answered in *The Descent of Man*, Charles Darwin's latest blockbuster, which takes up where his best-selling *On the Origin of Species* left off.

~
REVIEWERS' COMMENTS
'*Another wonderful book from a master scientist*'
Thomas Huxley

'*This book is another terrible … good … read*'
The Archbishop of Canterbury

'*I couldn't have put it better myself*'
Alfred Russel Wallace

The Descent of Man explained that man was descended from a non-human ancestor and that the pointy bits on

your ears are the ancient tips of pointy ears. It also added another element to the theory of evolution by explaining that animals need to mate as well as eat and that some of their features evolve because they make them more attractive even if the same features get in the way of hunting down lunch.

A shocking experiment

Charles was friends with Michael Faraday, and used his electricity generator to give people electric shocks so that they pulled weird faces – all in the cause of science of course. It was part of the research for his latest book, *The Expression of Emotions in Man and Animals*. His dog, Bob, helped a lot too; Charles would draw Bob when he was hungry, angry, happy, and so on.

Charles discovered lots more too, like why plants move and the size of the smallest piece of meat a carnivorous plant can detect. (Which is one-millonth of a gram.)

Pets without legs

Charles's last book was all about earthworms. He loved them and had all sorts of fun giving them nice big stones to bury, going out at night to watch them do whatever worms do at night, putting them on the piano and playing his cello to them, even going to Stonehenge to see what they'd been up to for the last 4,000 years.

AS LONG AS HE DOESN'T WANT TO TAKE US FISHING!

He calculated that nearby worm populations on the Downs brought up 18 tons of earth per acre per year. Charles's study of worms showed the same general point that evolution did – that small changes can cause huge effects, given enough time.

One thing that made Charles similar to Galileo and Newton is that he tried to use mathematics to check his theories. When people said worms were too puny to do all the amazing things Charles said they did, he did sums to prove they weren't. Unfortunately, like Faraday, he was a bit rubbish at maths, and made some basic mistakes in the books he spent so long writing but, also like Faraday, he was fully aware of the importance in science of testing theories and making predictions.

Charles lived happily at Down House with his family, Bob and the worms for many years until, in 1882, he died after a heart attack. He was so dead famous by then that he was buried next to Isaac Newton in Westminster Abbey. Charles had changed the way people look at the Universe as much as Isaac had; from then on it was clear that the natural world wasn't a changeless one which had suddenly been created a few thousand years ago. He showed that it was constantly – though slowly – changing through time, as generation succeeded generation and slime turned into us.

CHARLES DARWIN
THAT WAS YOUR LIFE
Revolutionized:
biology

TOP DISCOVERY:
• theory of evolution by natural selection

NON-SCIENTIFIC INTEREST:
reading novels (but only ones with happy endings)

There was, however, a big gap in the theory of evolution, as Charles knew. In the *Origin of Species* he said, 'No one can say why the same peculiarity in different individuals ... is sometimes inherited and sometimes not so; why the child often reverts in certain characters to its grandfather...'

NO ONE BUT ME

GREGOR MENDEL AND HIS WELL-BRED PEAS

There's one big difference between Gregor Mendel and the rest of the scientists in this book – he wasn't dead famous until he was dead. Yet he's as important a biologist as Charles Darwin. Though they never met and Charles probably didn't read the few scientific reports Mendel sent him, together they unlocked the secrets of life and started modern biology.

Gregor was born in 1822 in Silesia, in what is now the Czech Republic. Though a little bit posher than Michael Faraday's, his family wasn't what you'd call rich or classy. Gregor's dad was a very gloomy fruit-farmer, who became even gloomier when it became clear that Gregor (or Johann as he was then called, but let's call him Gregor anyway) had no interest in taking over the family business. Luckily Mrs Mendel was very jolly, which kind of made up for things, but still Gregor wasn't a happy child. When things got difficult he would become ill and go to bed – sometimes for months. Like Charles, his illness was probably psychological.

Gregor's parents were determined to make whatever sacrifices they had to to get him some kind of an education. But they couldn't afford to send him to school for long. On top of that, Silesia was a Catholic country that didn't encourage scientific debate. So it wasn't a very promising place to become a dead famous scientist, especially for someone as shy as Gregor.

Luckily, Gregor had a great teacher called Mr Schreiber. Mr Schreiber, like a lot of people in Silesia, was into fruit, especially apples. He even started an apple association and he succeeded where Mr Mendel had failed in getting Gregor interested in plants. He even taught Gregor how to breed them, which was to turn out to be very handy later on.

Gregor Czechs out

Mr Schreiber made sure that Gregor went on to a good secondary school at Opava. Unfortunately Opava was 36 km away, which meant he had to move. His parents could only afford to pay for half-board, so, to make ends meet, Gregor, aged 12, started to tutor other students.

This all made Mr M gloomier than ever since it meant there was no way Gregor could help on the farm now. Things got worse in 1838 when he injured himself. Gregor went home to help out…

Gregor stayed ill in bed for several months but, despite this interruption, he did OK at school and found he was good at tutoring. So he decided to become a teacher.

After six years he was ready to move on to the Philosophical Institute, 70 km away, where he needed to go to become a properly qualified teacher. The trouble was, he couldn't find another tutoring job to pay for it, so he went home again – and again spent most of the time in bed.

THIS IS GETTING VERY TEDIOUS

The next year, 1841, he did manage to find a tutoring job, and enrolled at the Institute. The problem was that the language in the area was Czech, not German as in Opava, and Gregor only knew a bit of Czech. He also had no friends and very little money. Then, just as everything seemed hopeless...

They got a lot worse. Gregor became ill again and went home to bed for a year.

If at first you don't succeed, get a habit

Gregor was rescued from his miserable existence by his nice younger sister, who generously offered him some of the money she'd got from her husband's family. This meant he could afford to continue at the Philosophical Institute, specializing in maths and physics and getting more and more into science. In fact, he wanted to be a scientist, and he decided to go to university to become one.

So all was finally well. Or it would have been if he'd had any money. But he didn't. So he couldn't go to university after all.

There was only one thing for it :

This may seem a rather odd move for someone who wanted to be a scientist, but at the time the local monasteries were quite like universities, with added praying – although Gregor didn't take that bit too seriously. Gregor's physics teacher recommended him in glowing terms. Well, fairly glowing – he said Gregor was 'almost the best' of his students. But that was good enough for Abbott Napp, head of St Thomas's Monastery in nearby Brünn. So, in 1843, aged 21, Gregor started at St Thomas's, which meant:

- he was assigned the name Gregor
- he was on his way to being dead famous at last
- his dad gave up all hope of him ever becoming a farmer.

Holy Mendel

In 1848, Gregor 'took holy orders', which meant he became a proper priest. It also gave him a duty he hated – visiting ill, dying, poor and otherwise badly-off people. He was OK at the job, but found it so depressing that he ended up in bed for a month.

Abbott Napp rescued him, allowing him to be a supply teacher of maths and classics. Gregor was still keen to become a fully-qualified teacher as well as a scientist but to do this he needed to pass an exam – which should have been easy for him. But his nerves got the better of him and he failed.

However, one of the examiners either spotted a lurking bit of genius in Gregor or felt sorry for him, and suggested to Napp that Gregor should be allowed – and funded – to study science full-time at Vienna University. It was a real bit of luck at last, and about time too. So in 1852, Gregor, aged 29, still a monk, and by a very roundabout route indeed, started his university course. As Napp said, 'He'd have made a very bad parish priest anyway.'

Trouble with mice

Despite having to work seven days a week, Gregor had a great time at university, studying physics and botany. Being shy, relatively ancient and a monk meant he didn't do many studenty things.

But he did find an exciting hobby: buying lottery tickets. Gregor really loved maths by now and anything to do with numbers fascinated him. And there was always that chance of becoming a rollover lottery jackpot millionaire.

Maybe it was at Vienna that Gregor decided to follow in the footsteps of Galileo and Newton and reduce the Universe to mathematical laws. Anyway, he learnt a lot and when he returned to the monastery in 1853, he had all the training he needed to do something amazing. And Napp had an amazing project all lined up for him.

Abbot Napp was fascinated by the question 'What is inherited and how?', and he was convinced that the only way to answer it was through experimental science. From then on, Gregor was in for a busy time; apart from lots of research and lots of reading, he taught 27 hours per week, prayed at least twice a day and ate gigantic breakfasts, lunches and dinners.

If you've been reading this book carefully (rather than just, say, leafing through it at the dentist's), you might be a little bit puzzled by now – if the Catholic Church was so anti-science, how come the monasteries were allowed to be scientific? It's because monasteries were powerful little places in those days, and they didn't always do what they were told. So, though the local bishop wasn't at all pleased with the disobedient monasteries and often moaned at Abbot Napp, Napp usually got his own way.

One thing the bishop moaned about was Gregor. This was partly because Gregor tended to be a bit sarcastic, and partly because he was doing experiments (nothing painful though) on mice. The bishop decided that was far too exciting for a young monk, so Gregor started to work on peas instead.

Gregor probably started his work on peas in 1854. He was doing some real science at last.

Parenting for peas

There's an annoying thing about our lack of knowledge about Gregor; it's not at all clear just why he worked on peas – was it his own idea or Napp's? Whoever had the idea was either very lucky or very clever, because peas turned out to be just the right vegetable to make Gregor dead famous.

It's not only unknown when Gregor started to work on peas or whose idea it was – it's not even clear exactly what he had in mind, despite the fact that he wrote some scientific papers on the subject. It's possible that he was simply trying to breed better peas. He could have been testing a theory of his own about inheritance. He could have been trying to solve the mysteries of evolution. Or maybe he was just doing what Napp told him. Anyway, before we go any further, it's time to meet the peas.

The way peas and other living things pass on their characteristics to their offspring was completely misunderstood by Charles Darwin and most other scientists of the time. They thought that children always inherited the averaged-out qualities of their parents – so breeding white flowers with red flowers should produce pink flowers. This is called Blending Inheritance and it was a huge problem for Charles's theory of evolution. And this is why...

The tail of Reggie Rabbit

Let's say one day a rabbit called Reggie is born with a really fantastic tail. A tail that can open tins, conduct orchestras, double as an attractive scarf, and knock foxes for six. A tail you can really hang your hat on.

According to Charles, Reggie – thanks to his wonderful tail – will scare off the foxes, get all the best grass, and survive to settle down with a nice female rabbit called Rachel and have a family of little rabbits called Ralph, Rastus, Raj and Rita.

Still according to Charles, the little rabbits will all have tails a bit like Reggie's – but also a bit like Rachel's. Fairly exciting tails, but not *brilliant*. And when the little rabbits have little rabbits of their own, their tails will be even less exciting, until, a few generations later, all that's left of Reggie's tail is a bedtime story for little bunnies.

Now what actually happens – at least in many cases – isn't like that at all. There's a good chance that Raj and Rita will have tails just like Reggie, while Ralph and Rastus will have tails just like Rachel.

In that case, Raj and Rita probably survive to give Reggie and Rachel grandchildren, while Ralph and Rastus get eaten by foxes (and are jolly tasty too, I expect), so Rachel and Reggie's grandbunnies have a good chance of having plenty of wonder-tails between them. The ones that do have a tail to brag about go on to breed, the ones that don't, don't, and before you know where you are all rabbits have tails like Reggie and are consequently top animal.

Properties in pairs

Gregor was very lucky, or clever – or someone was – to choose peas to study because pea plants occur in just two heights: around 200 cm and around 40 cm. Taking two peas, one tall, one short, let's say they make four new pea plants. How high do you reckon they will be:

a) All 200 cm? b) All 40 cm? c) All 120 cm?

d) A mix of 40 cm and 200 cm?

The right answer is d). Which is weird, isn't it? But Gregor knew just how to sort it all out.

5. BREED A PURE SHORT PEA PLANT WITH A PURE LONG ONE.

OOOH, YOU'RE JUST SO STRANGE AND EXOTIC LOOKING!

6. COUNT HOW MANY OF THE OFFSPRING ARE SHORT AND HOW MANY ARE LONG.

LONG, LONG, SHORT, LONG, SHORT, SHORT, SHORT, LONG, LONG, SHORT, LONG, LONG,

7. DO THIS WITH AT LEAST 15,000 MORE PEA PLANTS.

8. DO SOME SUMS.

9. BECOME DEAD FAMOUS.

Science Today

MENDEL HAILED AS A GENIUS!

122

After several years of this, Gregor found…

It wasn't just height that Gregor investigated but six other features too, and each time he got the same simple answer.

The reason – though Gregor didn't know it – is that each pea contains a pair of structures called alleles. Each allele can be a 'short' or a 'tall'. If the pea has a pair of 'shorts' … that is, two 'short' alleles, it will be short. If it has two 'tall' alleles it will be tall. If it has one of each it will be tall, because the 'tall' allele is stronger – more dominant – that the 'short' one.

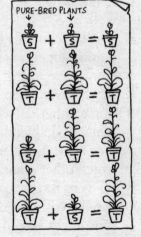

When two peas breed to produce a new pea plant, it will inherit a pair of height alleles. It gets one from each of its parents, completely randomly.

These few facts – alleles in pairs, one dominant, children take one from each parent randomly – formed the basis of a whole new science: genetics.

┌───┐
│ # SECRETS OF SCIENCE
│ Mendelian genetics explains just what is inherited
│ and why. It can be used to produce better crops,
│ healthier animals and to explain why your Aunt
│ Edna has such a big nose.
└───┘

Charles and Gregor

The picture Gregor ended up with was really very simple – characteristics are inherited according to a simple numerical ratio – and it might seem strange that he was the first to come up with it; after all, farmers had been breeding hybrid plants by crossing different varieties for thousands of years. And why hadn't Charles Darwin come up with the answer after all those years of fact collecting?

Well...

- The law can only be clearly seen with big numbers of plants: not *every* fourth pea will be short.
- These experiments take a long time – many generations of whatever creature you're experimenting on.
- Some inherited characteristics, like skin colour in humans, do blend, just as Charles thought.
- It's very difficult to control which plant breeds with which other plant.
- It's very tough to know for sure when you've got a pure breed to experiment on – a whole generation of peas might be tall just through chance, not because their parents are pure.
- Some characteristics are invisible, even with a microscope.

There are a lot more subtle problems too; some characteristics are shaped by more than one inherited factor, some characteristics are always passed on together, and there are weird things called 'hybrid vigour' and 'inbreeding weakness'.

In hybrid vigour a cross between a tall and small plant produces, not a medium one as Charles would have thought, nor a tall or a short one as Gregor's theory would imply, but a super-tall one. In inbreeding weakness, two closely related parents produce a weak baby (which is why you're not allowed to marry your relatives).

Gregor couldn't explain these things but genetics, the science he founded, could. And he could explain some things completely – such as why some brown-eyed parents only ever have brown-eyed children, while others sometimes have blue-eyed children. And why pairs of blue-eyed parents only ever have blue-eyed children.

Charles Darwin was fascinated by the diversity and complexity of nature so he had the wrong temperament to see the simple laws it obeyed. Gregor, on the other hand, was content to focus all his attention on one simple experiment. Charles had been useless at maths, so he wouldn't have looked for a mathematical law or found one if he had looked for it. Gregor succeeded where Charles failed because of his mathematical skill and because he approached the problem like Newton did – looking for the underlying simplicity behind the mass of complex details.

Gregor had a little break from peas in 1856, when he tried once more to get fully qualified as a teacher and … well, let's just draw a veil over that. Suffice to say he retired to bed for a long time. This was a real pity, because Gregor enjoyed teaching science, though his teaching methods were a bit unusual. He'd open a book at random, look at the page number, do a sum – like doubling it – and call on the student with that number. And then throw peas at them if they were naughty.

In 1862, Gregor made a brief trip to London to attend a technological exhibition, but mostly he just stayed at the monastery, breeding peas, counting them and lecturing to his students.

Too good to be true?

Gregor's results were good. Really good. In fact, they seem too good to be true. If you did what Gregor did and counted how many of 4,000 pea plants were short, you'd expect to find about 1,000. But you'd be very surprised to find *exactly* 1,000. Though Gregor's results weren't quite that perfect, they were suspiciously close. It's been calculated that the chances of him getting such good results without cheating are 10,000 to 1. So what happened? *Did* he cheat? Maybe, or maybe one of the other monks who assisted him was responsible, but no one really knows.

By 1865, Gregor had bred and counted enough peas. It was time to make his results public. So, one snowy evening, he made his way to the school where he taught and gave the first of two lectures to the Brünn Society for the Study of Natural Sciences. About 40 people were there, including some quite senior botanists. At the end of his talk he left plenty of space for questions. But…

One month later he gave another lecture. This time…

Gregor must have been bitterly disappointed. All those years of work had resulted in a crucial insight into the way inheritance worked, an insight that could explain why plants and animals and people were the way they were. And though that insight was now public, no one understood, no one cared, no one even listened.

Gregor didn't give up. But it was time to move on from peas, to discover whether the law he'd found was general and applied to other living things. So he investigated several other types of plant and also bees, though only one investigation – of beans – was completed to the point where he published a paper. There were several reasons for this, one was the enormous amount of time it took to breed the plants, and another was because he spent most of his time studying the wrong thing. Another sad episode in Gregor's life was about to begin.

The hawkweed horror

To start with, Gregor published his pea lectures in the journal of the Brünn Society. Next, he ordered 40 copies and sent at least 12 of them off to scientists all over the world, including Charles Darwin. Then he waited to see what other scientists would say about his discovery. Would they love it or hate it?

They ignored it. He only got a single letter in response, from a top botanist called Karl von Nägeli. Karl wasn't too impressed, having completely missed the point of the paper. However, for Gregor, the letter from Nägeli meant contact with another scientist at last. For all scientists (except Isaac Newton) success means that your discoveries are understood and accepted by other scientists, so the letter meant a great deal to him.

Gregor wrote a nice letter back, explaining his theory in more detail, but Nägeli didn't reply. He didn't reply to Gregor's next letter either. In fact, it was only three letters later, when Gregor humbly asked Nägeli if he had any suggestions for further research work, that Nägeli wrote back, suggesting the species Gregor should investigate next: the hawkweed.

Actually, Gregor could have studied almost any type of plant or animal to confirm his theory (though some would have been easier than others).

Any species with parents that interbreed normally, in fact. Unlike, say ... the hawkweed.

Abbot Mendel

Gregor might have gone on to experiment on other plants or animals, but in 1868 Abbot Napp died. Gregor was elected as abbot in his place, and that meant a whole new lot of responsibilities for the next 16 years:

> ## Gregor Mendel
> *Abbot, St Thomas's Monastery*
> *Director, Moravian Mortgage Bank*
> *Member, Royal and Imperial Order*
> *of Francis Joseph*
> *Curator, Moravian Institute for Deaf Mutes*

He spent most of what free time he had arguing with the authorities about the high taxes the monastery was made to pay. He must have spent quite a lot of time eating too since, as he put it:

> *I am no longer well fitted for botanical expeditions, seeing that Heaven has blessed me with an excess of avoirdupois [weight], and this makes long walks and especially hill-climbing very difficult for me in a world where universal gravitation prevails.*

But Gregor's last years weren't too miserable, despite the lack of science. In return for his sister's financial support in getting an education he had agreed to look after her three sons, and they stayed friends for the rest of his life, going for walks and playing chess together. He also collected funny stories and played practical jokes.

He had faith that the value of his work would be recognized one day: 'My time will come,' he said. And so it did. In 1900, his long-forgotten published papers were discovered by three biologists. They recognized what a breakthrough he had made and rushed off to tell the world about Gregor's work. So, as the twentieth century began, he finally did become … DEAD FAMOUS. Sadly, by then he'd been dead for 16 years.

GREGOR MENDEL
THAT WAS YOUR LIFE
Revolutionized:
biology

TOP DISCOVERY:
• genetics

NON-SCIENTIFIC INTEREST:
lunch

One thing which stopped Gregor from being dead famous sooner was that he was no good at marketing himself. Which is not something you could *possibly* say about Louis Pasteur…

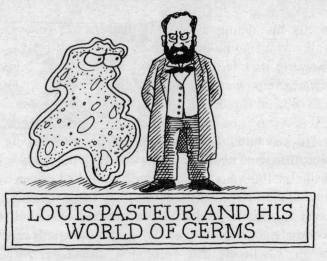

LOUIS PASTEUR AND HIS WORLD OF GERMS

Louis Pasteur was one of the greatest scientists of all. He was also one of the most unpleasant. He was born in eastern France in 1822, only a few months after Gregor.

In those days, things were OK if you were healthy and wealthy, but if you were poor or ill they were grim. A lot of people lived in slums and a lot of people died young, especially when one of the frequent epidemics was raging through the country: flu, smallpox, cholera, French military fever.

FLU   SMALLPOX   CHOLERA   FRENCH MILITARY FEVER

FEVER, ACHES, EXHAUSTION   SICKNESS, CRAMPS IN LEGS, BELLY   SEVERE DIARRHOEA CRAMPS

If you were very ill you went to hospital, where the chances were you'd be dead in a few weeks, having been infected by the doctors or the other patients. The trouble was, no one understood that diseases were spread by germs. Some thought it was God's punishment when they fell ill, while slightly more scientific people thought diseases were spread by bad smells. (So not a lot more scientific, in fact.)

Though no one knew what caused diseases, that didn't stop doctors claiming they could cure them – the cure for rabies involved being branded with red-hot pokers, being bled, having your wounds constantly kept open and having salt and vinegar rubbed into them. It's said that Louis witnessed this treatment as a child, so it's not very surprising that he hated physicians for the rest of his life, especially when he discovered how wrong they were.

Louis' dad was a leather-maker. As a child, Louis was about as interested in science as he was in leather-making – which was not very. What he liked was drawing, and he was really good at it. The people he drew and painted were apparently a bit of a glum lot, since not one of them is smiling in the pictures that survive. In fact, fun seems to have been rather an alien concept to Louis when he was a nipper, and when he grew up he got even more serious.

In 1842, Louis took the exam to enter the best school around – the École Normale Supérieur, in Paris. He passed, coming 15th in his class of 22. You might think he'd rush excitedly to Paris to learn things, and so he did, but not to the École. He reckoned coming 15th just wasn't good enough, so he went to boarding school instead, to prepare to re-sit the entrance exam. The next year he tried again and came fourth. Though none too pleased, he supposed that would have to do, and off he went to the École.

Over the next few years, Louis studied like crazy and in 1847 he became a Doctor of Science. The next year he invented a new science.

The handy Universe

Louis liked crystals, maybe because they're so stylish. At the time there was a bit of a mystery about a pair of crystalline substances called tartaric acid and racemic acid. Chemically, they're just the same – they have the same properties and are made out of the same amounts of the same things. But something odd happens when they are dissolved in water; if you shine a beam of light through a solution of tartaric acid, the light beam twists clockwise. But racemic acid doesn't affect light at all.

Louis decided to study the relatively dull and boring racemic acid rather than the weird and groovy tartaric sort. These days – and then too, to some extent – chemical analysis is all about sensitive machines, chemical tests and lots of calculations. Louis, on the other hand, used a really big magnifying glass. He looked long and carefully at his pile of little crystals and, after a while, he noticed something a bit odd.

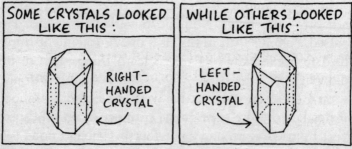

Excitedly, Louis reached for a little teeny-tiny pair of tweezers. He sorted the crystals into the two types, dissolved each in water and shone light beams through them. One light beam twisted clockwise, indicating the presence of tartaric acid – and the other twisted anticlockwise! Not only had he made tartaric acid out of racemic acid, he'd invented a new substance, linked chemistry to light *and* launched a new science – stereochemistry, the study of the three-dimensional shapes of molecules.

It's said that Louis was so excited he rushed out and hugged the first person he saw (history doesn't record who this lucky person was) before dragging him into his laboratory to show him his crystals. His physicist friend Jean Baptiste Biot (who *must* have been dead famous at the time for his incredible comb-over) supposedly said, 'My dear child, I have all my life so loved this science that I can hear my heart beat for joy.' Maybe people really talked like that in those days.

Being a genius already, Louis soon understood some of the implications of his discovery:

Louis' Lost Book of Secrets
Crystals are made of molecules and the shapes of the molecules control the shapes of the crystals.
Since the shape of crystals affects light as I've just brilliantly proved, that means, armed with my stunning intellect, I can work out their molecular shapes, simply by the way the crystals affect light!
Sacré bleu! It's the discovery of a genius!

Later...
I have made an amazing discovery that surprises even me. All living things are made of asymmetric molecules - that is, molecules which can exist in either left- or right-handed forms.
Another triumph for Louis Pasteur! My name will live in history!
Ahahahahaha...

SECRETS OF SCIENCE

Louis' idea that left- and right-handedness is a key to understanding living matter is quite correct. Not only does the handedness of chemicals affect their smells and tastes and make them edible or not, subatomic particles also have types of handedness and this played a big part in the way matter formed from energy in the early Universe.

On the strength of his discovery, in 1849, still only 27, Louis became lecturer in Chemistry at Strasbourg University. But, like Michael Faraday, he moved away from chemistry after a while, in his case to biology.

The same year he met and married one of the daughters of the Principal, Marie Laurent. She was an unusual person. She was completely devoted to Louis and worked with him often, despite the fact that he hardly spoke to her – for him work came first and everything else came about nineteenth. So he wasn't exactly a fun person – of all the hundreds of paintings, photos, sculptures and drawings of him, only one shows him smiling.

Louis and Marie had five children but, as often happened in those days, three died in childhood, two of typhoid.

Beetroot bugs

In 1854, Louis became Professor of Chemistry at the University of Lille in northern France. Lille was the main place in France where alcohol was made from beetroot juice. But the juice often turned vinegary instead of alcoholic. Monsieur Bigo, a big noise in the world of beetroot, asked Louis to help, and Louis, armed with his trusty microscope, did. He took samples of the healthy and unhealthy juices and compared them.

The healthy juice was full of globules of yeast. It was known at the time that yeast was needed to make things ferment; it was thought that the fermentation was a chemical reaction resulting from the breakdown of the yeast. The unhealthy juice was full of what looked like wriggling black rods which looked very lively to Louis.

Louis' massive brain kicked into gear – could it be that both yeast and the black rods were actually living things? If that was the case, perhaps the life processes of yeast produced nice alcohol while those of the rods produced nasty vinegary acid?

Louis experimented with the yeast particles and the black rods and found that they could reproduce; so they really were alive. Louis told Monsieur Bigo that he should look for the black rods and, when he found them, chuck away that batch of juice. Bigo did as he was told and the alcohol industry was saved! Louis became a local hero.

The idea that microbes were somehow linked to disease wasn't new, but people thought they were *produced* by disease, not that they caused it. This might seem a weird thing to think, and that's why we have to have a little look at...

How to create life

Aristotle thought that living things could appear whenever moist things became dry or whenever dry things became moist. Though a lot of people, not surprisingly, thought this a little OTT, until a few centuries ago they did believe that all sorts of creatures appeared from non-living matter – frogs from slime, maggots from meat, even eels from river mud and mice from grain. Gradually scientists disproved these theories, but in Louis' time it was still thought that microbes – which had been discovered in the late seventeenth century – were spontaneously created, even if other things weren't. Louis was an avid Catholic and he thought that such theories (as well as Charles Darwin's ideas) were complete nonsense; only God could make life.

Louis' political ideas may have helped him come up with his theory:

Louis' Lost Book of Secrets

Rant number 239

Pah! I hate democracy! This stupid idea that everyone is as good as everyone else! As good as Pasteur? Down with common people, that's what I say... dirty, stubby little individuals.

(Hmmm... reminds me of microbes.) They're a menace to society and need to be kept firmly under control. Give them the chance and they'll have loads of kids. (Just like germs multiplying!) And stop society working properly. (Like the body, when it's ill.) The only thing they've good for is being servants and tidying up after people like me. (As germs are good for breaking down dead things.) I feel another world-shaking triumph of science coming on...

Anyway, whatever the reason, Louis was sure that the world was full of disease-carrying germs travelling through the air on dust. He was absolutely right – the germ theory of disease was a complete success. He proved it, with a bit of broth, like this:

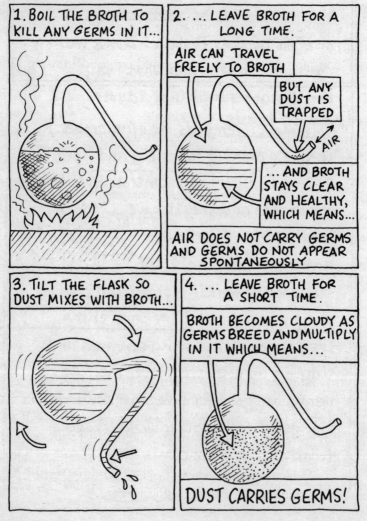

1. BOIL THE BROTH TO KILL ANY GERMS IN IT...

2. ...LEAVE BROTH FOR A LONG TIME.

AIR CAN TRAVEL FREELY TO BROTH

BUT ANY DUST IS TRAPPED

AIR

...AND BROTH STAYS CLEAR AND HEALTHY, WHICH MEANS...

AIR DOES NOT CARRY GERMS AND GERMS DO NOT APPEAR SPONTANEOUSLY

3. TILT THE FLASK SO DUST MIXES WITH BROTH...

4. ...LEAVE BROTH FOR A SHORT TIME.

BROTH BECOMES CLOUDY AS GERMS BREED AND MULTIPLY IN IT WHICH MEANS...

DUST CARRIES GERMS!

Some of the flasks are kept in a French museum and are still clear to this day.

SECRETS OF SCIENCE

Though Louis was not – as he implied – the inventor of the theory that each disease is caused and spread by a particular type of germ, his experiments helped to prove that it was correct and opened the way for the conquest of diseases, many cured by Louis himself.

Tea with Louis

Tea with the Pasteurs wasn't really much fun. It would go like this:

Louis' Teatime Timetable

16:30 Arrive for tea. Louis refuses to shake your hand in case he catches something.

16:40 Louis starts to clean the clean glasses.

16:50 Soup and bread arrive. Louis starts to take his bread roll apart.

17:00 Bread now in crumbs, surrounded by little piles of the things Louis has found in it – bits of spider, wool, cockroach etc.

17:05 Main course arrives: rabbit. Louis talks about his latest experiments – cutting up rabbits, drying their brains, how difficult it is to get the nerves out of their spines, especially when the rabbits are still alive, and how he really much prefers to get someone else to do the job for him.

17:20 Dessert. Tirade from Louis about how terrible foreigners, homosexuals and lefties are.

Oh yes, and don't take any German wine with you… Louis hated anything to do with Germany (or rather Prussia, as the biggest chunk of it was then called).

Being ever so patriotic, Louis was very pleased to accept the Emperor's request to travel to Arbois near the Swiss border to study wine diseases. In 1864 he went there and again showed that microbes were responsible for causing sourness in wine. And this time he discovered how to cure it – by heating it briefly, a process he later applied to lots of other drinks and which is now called pasteurization.

The same year, a worldwide silkworm plague which had started in China in 1849 reached France, and Louis was asked by the Government to see if he could sort it out. Though by now very confident of the success of his theories, he wasn't too sure about how to apply them to animals, and he'd never even seen a silkworm. But he went and studied the sickly silkworms anyway, and decided that the disease must be passed on by their eggs. He advised the breeders only to use eggs from healthy silkworms and to destroy the rest.

Sadly, it didn't work – even the eggs of healthy silkworms hatched into worms which died. The industry was very cross indeed, until Louis discovered that the droppings of the silkworms could spread the disease too. Hurrah! *Another* industry saved, and another promotion for Louis – to become Professor of Chemistry at the Sorbonne, the Paris university where he'd once attended lectures.

By this time, Louis' ideas were spreading abroad, and in England Joseph Lister, convinced of the correctness of the germ theory of disease, discovered a way of destroying germs without pasteurization – by using carbolic acid to clean wounds and hands. Soon, Louis' discoveries had saved more lives than those of any other scientist.

Louis himself was a healthy bloke on the whole, until 1868. On 19 October, the day he was supposed to give an important scientific lecture, Louis had a stroke. It was expected that he would die, or at least give up work. However, within a few months he was back at work, making a trip to London to help with a beer-souring problem. His stroke didn't hold him back, though it made him even more irritable than before. Which was unfortunate, since some very irritating things were about to happen.

In 1871, France lost the Franco-Prussian war. Louis was so annoyed he swore he'd begin all his future scientific publications with the words 'Hatred toward Prussia. Revenge! Revenge!' He also hated the fact that he hadn't actually proved his germ theory – germs were clearly associated with disease but was it really true that each disease was caused by a different germ? Worse still, when the theory was finally proved it wasn't by Louis, but by a Prussian, Robert Koch.

Louis's lucky chicken

In 1878, Louis and his assistant invented ... an indestructible chicken! (At least as far as chicken cholera was concerned.)

What had happened was that the weakened germs, though not strong enough to kill, had triggered the chicken's natural defences, and its body had managed to come up with a cure for the cholera, which was then effective against the full-strength version of the disease. Louis and other scientists used the same idea (known as vaccination) to protect people against other diseases – polio, tetanus, chickenpox, measles...

> # SECRETS OF SCIENCE
> The idea of vaccinating people by injecting them with weakened versions of deadly diseases to enable their own bodies to find a cure has saved millions of lives.

The first of these many successes was against anthrax, the disease that Robert Koch had used to prove the germ theory was correct. After some experiments with weakened anthrax germs, Louis was challenged in 1881 to provide a public demonstration. Though his work was still far from complete, he couldn't resist; on 5 May he and his assistant inoculated half of a group of sheep, goats and cows with weakened anthrax. On 17 May they inoculated them again and on 31 May both the inoculated and non-inoculated animals were injected with what would normally be a lethal dose. All the inoculated animals survived, while the non-inoculated ones died. Louis had triumphed over yet another deadly disease, saving countless more lives in the generations to come.

Robert Koch wasn't best pleased with Louis, who hadn't mentioned him in his reports on the disease. Then, at an international conference in Switzerland, Louis gave him a jolly good shouting at and in response

Koch published papers showing that Louis's work was inadequately prepared; because he didn't know how to control the strength of the weakened germs, some were too weak to provide any protection and others were so strong they actually infected healthy animals.

Much later it was discovered that Louis also deceived everyone about the way he prepared the vaccine. A scientist called Jean-Jacques Toussaint had actually suggested the basis of the method to Louis. But Louis never mentioned this, implying instead that a quite different method was used, one that he'd invented himself. This meant he got all the fame and huge piles of cash, too. Meanwhile, Jean-Jacques remained poor and had a nervous breakdown within a year.

The rabid rabbits

One of the scariest diseases at the time was rabies. Its terrible effects on the minds of its victims suggested that the brain was contaminated, so Louis tried infecting dogs with rabies and then curing them with bits of dried brain from rabid rabbits. It was very risky work, and Louis courageously exposed himself to the risk of infection many  times – but it was a brilliant success. According to Louis.

The obvious next step was to test the cure on people. But injecting people with any sort of rabies, weakened or not, was terribly risky. However, in 1885 a boy called Joseph Meister was brought to Louis by his mother –

he'd been bitten fourteen times by a rabid dog. Since it seemed he was certain to develop rabies – and if he did he'd certainly die – it seemed Louis had nothing to lose, and he injected Joseph with his rabies cure. Joseph remained healthy and Louis became even more rich and famous than he was already (which was very).

However when Louis' notebooks were released a century later they revealed that the true story wasn't quite so simple; for one thing, although about 60% of the dogs Louis had treated survived, about the same percentage of untreated ones survived too. For another, the method he used on Joseph was actually not the same as the one he'd used on the dogs (he only tested it on them later). And finally, Joseph might well have survived even if he'd been left alone: people bitten by rabid dogs often don't develop rabies. So Louis *could* have infected a healthy person with a deadly, incurable disease.

But Louis was lucky. And so was Joseph.

LUCKY? I GET BITTEN FOURTEEN TIMES BY A RABID DOG AND THEN EXPERIMENTED ON BY LOONY LOUIS PASTEUR AND YOU'RE CALLING ME **LUCKY**?

None of this was known at the time; Louis was a hero and in 1888 an international institute for research and teaching, the Pasteur Institute, was opened by the French Academy of Sciences. Louis was its first director, rather terrifyingly for the staff since he was so strict and scary.

During his life Louis kept his notebooks secret, and instructed that they stay that way after his death. Presumably he couldn't bring himself to destroy them. His instructions were obeyed from his death in 1895 until 1971, when his last direct male descendant died. It was those notebooks which revealed that Louis was not quite the all-round wonderful human being people used to think he was. On the other hand, thanks to his work – and to that same domineering personality that made him so unpleasant – millions of people who would have died of terrible diseases survived. He may well have saved more lives than anyone else, before or since.

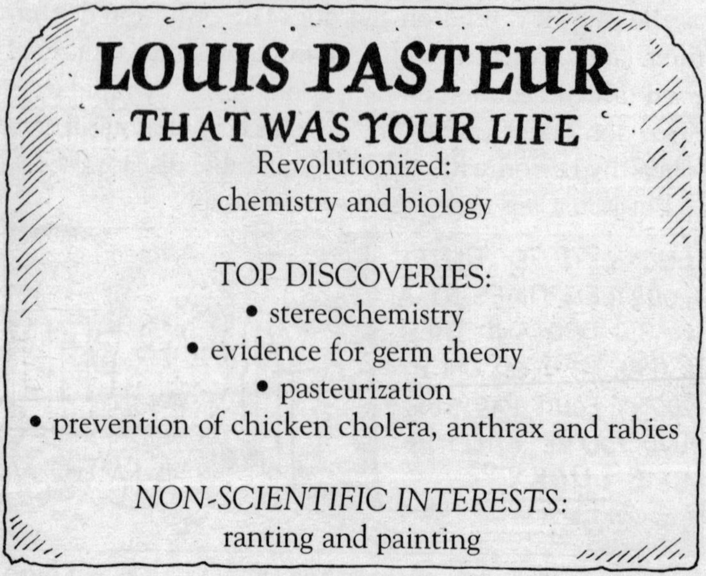

LOUIS PASTEUR
THAT WAS YOUR LIFE
Revolutionized:
chemistry and biology

TOP DISCOVERIES:
- stereochemistry
- evidence for germ theory
- pasteurization
- prevention of chicken cholera, anthrax and rabies

NON-SCIENTIFIC INTERESTS:
ranting and painting

MARIE CURIE AND HER DEATH-RAYS

More than one scientist in this book suffered because of their discoveries…

…but only Marie Curie was actually killed off by them. She really did give her life to science…

Marie (then called Maria) Salomea Sklodowska was born in Warsaw, in what is now Poland, in 1867, the year Michael Faraday died. She was one of five clever children and two clever parents, both of whom were teachers. Even the games she and her sisters and brother played were brainy; there was complicated poetry, a historical collage, and geographical building blocks. But Marie was clever even by the standards of her family – when she was four, she took a book that her six-year-old sister was struggling to read, and read it correctly – out loud.

Marie's family was close and fun-loving as well as amazingly bright, but at that time there was a lot of illness and death about, just as Charles Darwin and Louis Pasteur had found. Marie's sister Zosia died young and, when Marie was ten her mother died too, of tuberculosis.

Marie was always top of the class at school even though she was two years younger than her classmates. Weirdly enough, a lot of their lessons were actually forbidden. This was because in 1867 there was no such place as Poland; the area was controlled by different countries and Warsaw was controlled by the Russians who wanted everyone to speak Russian, and kept a close eye and a big ear on them to make sure they did.

This meant that Marie and her friends had to pretend they were learning authorized subjects in Russian when in fact they were learning illegal stuff in Polish; so when, according to the timetable, Marie was learning home economics and botany, she was really studying Polish history and German. Scarily, every so often the Russian government would send an inspector to check up on the pupils by asking them fiendishly tricky questions in Russian. Marie was always chosen to answer and usually got them all right.

Despite being rather an odd place, Marie's school was a good one and she was happy there. But then, in about 1878, she was transferred to a new school because – so it's said – her father thought it would be a challenge that would help her get over her mother's recent death. And a challenge it certainly was; the teachers were Russian – and not very nice. They weren't very good either, having been selected for their jobs because of their patriotism, not their brains. Marie was probably expecting to get straight As as usual, but one of her teachers refused to give her any more than a C. He used to say, 'Only God deserves an A and the B is reserved for me.' Which must have been extremely annoying.

OH I DON'T KNOW,
SEEMS A GOOD
SYSTEM TO ME.

You may be thinking that Marie sounds a bit too good to be true, but she could be jolly lippy on occasion, and didn't take kindly to her nasty teachers.

So schooling wasn't much fun for Marie any more, and nor was the fact that her relatives were being polished off by a variety of diseases that Louis Pasteur's discoveries hadn't cured yet. She must have been very pleased, after she left school at 15, to stay with her relatives in the country for a year. She danced like crazy – attending a three-day dancing party and wearing through the soles of a new pair of shoes.

From then on she thought the countryside was brilliant and would visit it whenever she was ill or unhappy. On this first visit she and her cousin also enjoyed themselves by playing practical jokes on people

– such as gradually watering down someone's milk just to see when they'd notice, and even…

As soon as the holiday was over, Marie had to face a big problem. It was obvious that her head was stuffed to busting with high-power brains and that she should go to university to learn how to use them, but there was a difficulty. Marie was a girl. Girls were *not allowed* to go to university in Warsaw or almost anywhere else. The Sorbonne – Louis Pasteur's Parisian university – did accept female undergraduates, but there was no way Marie's family could afford to send her there.

The floating university

Luckily, in 1882, a group of Poles had started up a 'floating university' for young women like Marie. It was a secret network of people who organized lectures and tutorials all over the place.

In 1884, both Marie and her sister Bronia joined. The floating university, though a great help, couldn't award degrees. To get them, Marie and Bronia would just have to go to Paris. But how could they afford it? Soon they had formulated a cunning plan. Bronia would go to Paris for four years while Marie worked as a governess to support them both. Then she would join Bronia and get her own degree, while Bronia helped her. Which was great – for Bronia. Marie, aged 18, was soon on her way back to the Polish countryside to fulfil her side of the bargain by becoming a live-in governess.

Love and labs

To begin with, Marie quite liked the work. She not only taught the children of the family, she also gave free – and illegal – Polish lessons to local children and read up on lots of subjects herself. She soon discovered that she liked maths and physics best and her employer's children least. They were so *dumb*.

In about 1887, Marie fell in love with the son of the household, which would have been great except that her employers were dead against their relationship – she was far too poor for their son. As she said about her plans for a relationship with him: 'They have gone up in smoke; I have buried them; locked them up; sealed and forgotten them – for … walls are stronger than the heads which try to demolish them.'

Not surprisingly, Marie gradually became more and more miserable. But she didn't give up; she said her rule of life was to 'never let one's self be beaten down, by persons or by events'. So she struggled on until 1889 when she went back to Warsaw to stay with her dad for a year. During that year, her cousin gave her a brilliant present – the use of a laboratory. It was a bit rubbish really, with no atomic accelerators, electron sequencers or Bunsen burners, but she loved it and felt that she'd come home at last. From then on, the countryside was only her second-favourite place.

The perils of Paris

In 1891, Marie, now 23, joined Bronia and her husband Kazimierz in Paris. Unfortunately, she couldn't understand the French of the lecturers at the Sorbonne, she didn't get on that well with Kazimierz and she had very little money – Bronia and Kazimierz weren't exactly rich. After six months Marie moved out to a tiny unheated flat where she lived on tea and bread and butter and passed out from hunger and/or cold every so often.

Marie wasn't a very studenty kind of a student – she didn't dance, date, wear groovy clothes or get into politics or music. Studying gave her all the fun she needed, especially when she got the hang of the language. And since she could spend all her time at the Sorbonne studying, her years there were some of the happiest of her life.

Being a genius as well as a workaholic, it's no surprise that Marie was spectacularly successful and came first in her year at science in 1893. After a holiday in Poland which she mostly spent making up for all that bread and tea, she returned to the Sorbonne for a

second degree, in maths this time. She came second in her year.

A scientific romance

The same year, 1894, Marie met Pierre Curie, a shy young scientist whose favourite things were crystal symmetry (like Louis Pasteur), and magnetism (like Michael Faraday). He'd recently found that when he squeezed certain crystals they produced electricity, a discovery which led eventually to digital watches. Another of Pierre's discoveries was that he *really* liked Marie and she *really* liked him. Romantically, he sent her a scientific report he'd written about crystallographic phenomena. It was *exactly* the sort of gift that Marie liked.

After a few months, Pierre proposed. Marie was quite keen but somewhat put off by the fact that he wasn't Polish. So she went off to the countryside for a bit of a think. After a few letters from Pierre, no doubt full of lovey-dovey non-linear differential equations and complex polynomials, she accepted.

Kazimierz's mother offered to buy Marie a wedding dress, and Marie requested something nice and dark and practical for lab work.

Back in Paris, after their honeymoon, Marie looked for a subject she could study to be awarded a PhD. She wasn't a bit put off by the fact that not a single woman in Europe had ever been granted one.

One of the newest mysteries of science were X-rays, which can go right through most materials. They had been discovered in 1895 by Wilhelm Röntgen and could be used to look inside people without all the bother of slicing them open. In 1896, a scientist called Henri Becquerel discovered that the dense metal uranium gave off mysterious rays that were similar to X-rays.

Marie decided they sounded just the thing for her, so in 1897, pausing only to have a daughter called Irène, she began work. Having almost no money made it difficult, but she was granted the use of an old glassed-in storeroom at a school. Since the temperature ranged from 6°C to about 35°C and it was decidedly damp it wasn't ideal but, never mind, it was a laboratory, and that's what Marie loved.

The mystery element

Over the next few months, Marie investigated lots of different materials to find out whether they gave off the mysterious Becquerel rays or not, and in February 1898...

MARIE'S LOST LUMINOUS LAB BOOK

Page 16
What a shocker! I tested some pitchblende, the ore from which uranium is extracted, and it's FOUR times more active than uranium is!

It must contain some other active material, unknown to science. Or to anyone else for that matter.

Page 19
There's something incredible about this mysterious super-active substance. Its activity is the same whatever the chemical state of the pitchblende.

That means the source of the activity is not a chemical reaction. It can only be something from within the atom itself.

Blimey.

Marie had found a key to a new science – nuclear physics.

SECRETS OF SCIENCE

One of the major achievements of twentieth-century science was the development of nuclear physics: the understanding of the internal structure of atoms.

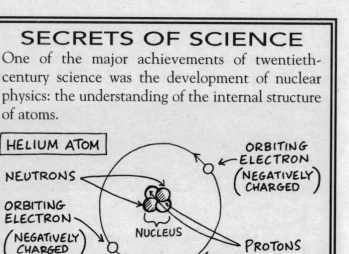

HELIUM ATOM

ORBITING ←ELECTRON
(NEGATIVELY CHARGED)

NEUTRONS

ORBITING ELECTRON
(NEGATIVELY CHARGED)

NUCLEUS

PROTONS
(POSITIVELY CHARGED)

Unlike the other scientists in this book, Marie wasn't much interested in the theoretical side of science. She wanted to find out about the Universe by experimenting, not theorizing, and the obvious next experiment was to separate out the mysterious radioactive substance from the pitchblende. Then she could study it properly.

MARIE'S LOST LUMINOUS LAB BOOK

Page 22
Pierre has begun to help me with my work. I'm determined to track down this weird substance, and I'm going to do it like this: I'll use chemical treatments

to separate pitchblende into a pair of substances that make it up. Then I'll test each member of the pair to see which is still producing radiation, and then separate that substance into another pair of substances, and again find in which member the mystery element is hiding.

Using this approach, Marie found that there were actually two sources of radioactivity present, and in 1898 she managed to track down one of them – a new element which she called polonium after her native Poland. When she announced it she used the word 'radioactivity' for the first time.

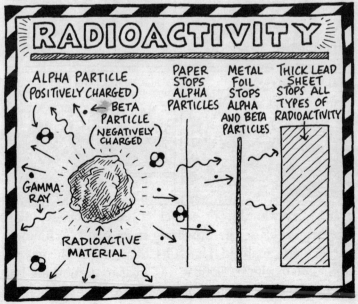

RADIOACTIVITY

ALPHA PARTICLE (POSITIVELY CHARGED)

BETA PARTICLE (NEGATIVELY CHARGED)

GAMMA RAY

RADIOACTIVE MATERIAL

PAPER STOPS ALPHA PARTICLES

METAL FOIL STOPS ALPHA AND BETA PARTICLES

THICK LEAD SHEET STOPS ALL TYPES OF RADIOACTIVITY

Later the same year, Marie and Pierre tracked down the second material, which they called radium.

But that wasn't the end of the story. Marie knew that what she and Pierre had actually found were substances which *contained* the two new elements. She hadn't isolated them in a pure form, and that's what she wanted to do next, especially the more radioactive one, radium.

Tough chemistry

Marie managed to find a slightly better laboratory – an old dissecting room. In early 1899 she got hold of a huge pile of pitchblende and she and Pierre started work.

It was very hard work – much of it done outside, in all weathers, because the dissecting room had no chimney. While Pierre analysed the results, Marie did all the muscle stuff. The Curies thought it was great to do nothing but science, to work together and to devote all their energies to tracking down the mysterious element. 'We lived in our single preoccupation as if in a dream,' Marie said.

Three years and ten months later, they had done it – they had extracted 0.1 of a gram of radium from over a million kilograms of pitchblende, and the element they found was even more amazing than they'd imagined. Unlike any other known metal, it generated heat and it *glowed*. When Marie and Pierre went into the laboratory one evening, they were astonished to see parts of it shining with eerie patches of blue-green light.

The destroying ray

Over the next few years, Marie and Pierre studied the weird properties of radium. They found it made glass cloudy and other things radioactive. It also burnt their hands. They didn't know that it was doing a lot more than that to them: by the end of 1902 they each had a collection of ailments, probably at least partly caused by their constant exposure to radioactivity. Deep inside their cells, even worse damage was being done.

SECRETS OF SCIENCE

Radioactivity damages living cells in many ways, and the destruction it causes can affect the way cells grow, leading to cancer or to changes passed on to children. These passed-on changes are called mutations and are almost always a disadvantage to the child. But occasionally the mutation can be an advantage in some way, in which case it has a good chance of being passed to succeeding generations, just as Darwin discovered and Mendel explained.

Oddly enough, the reaction of scientists to the discovery that radium could burn skin was not...

but...

because they thought it might be a cure for cancer. And so it is – in a way. Radioactivity destroys cancer cells, but it's not fussy and will destroy healthy cells too. So, when it is used to help deal with cancer, its destructive energies need to be aimed and contained very carefully indeed.

Doctor Curie

Eventually, Pierre got a lecturing job at the Sorbonne. After he was promoted to Professor of Physics there, Marie became Head of the Laboratory, the same job Michael Faraday had had at the Royal Institution. But the Curies' lives weren't all spent doing scientific kinds of things. Not *quite* all. Well, OK, actually they were, but not always in laboratories – they had scientific tea parties and a scientific cycling holiday too, to the Brittany coast. On this trip, another scientist called Paul Langevin went with them. This will turn out to be highly significant in a few pages...

In June 1903, Marie decided she was quite brilliant enough now to apply for her doctorate so she did, and got one with no problems. Paul Langevin gave a dinner party in her honour to celebrate. In December, Marie, Pierre, and Henri Becquerel were jointly given a special annual physics award – the Nobel Prize – for their work on radioactivity. The Nobel Prizes had been awarded in a variety of subjects since 1900 but Marie was the first woman to receive one (and her daughter was the second).

Suddenly, Marie was famous and appeared in all the papers. Marie's cat became a bit famous too, because Marie herself didn't have a lot to say and the reporters talked about it instead. She hated being even slightly well-known, saying, 'We must be interested in things, not people'.

One thing was as famous as Marie: radium. People were fascinated by its spooky glow and one dancer even had radium-impregnated clothes made to dance in. She came round and danced for Marie and Pierre and they became quite matey.

When it seemed that radium might cure all cancers, it became more famous still, not to mention pricier: already in 1903 it cost £400 a gram and would cost £20,000 a gram in 1918. Marie and Pierre could have patented the process of extraction, so that companies would have had to pay them a royalty for its use. But they thought this might hold back scientific progress, saying '…it would be against the scientific spirit'. Instead, they linked up with an industrial chemist in 1904 to get some money from the medical exploitation of radium. That same year, their second daughter, Éve, was born.

The next year, people started to use radium to try to cure cancer. Meanwhile, Marie and Pierre started to go to seances, to see if there was anything in spiritualism. Their medium, the brilliantly named Eusapia Palladino, had a hole in her head from which a cold wind blew when the spirits of the departed dropped by for a natter and a bit of a supernatural manifestation. Or so she said.

The crash

By now, things were going really well for the Curies – they had some major scientific discoveries to their credit, a bit of money, two daughters, and OK jobs. The only downsides were that they weren't too healthy and were very, very famous.

But then, in 1906…

Marie was completely stunned. She'd lost her best colleague and closest friend as well as her husband. She decided that all she could do was to keep on working, so after a month with her family she was back in the lab.

Soon, Bronia joined her. Marie was offered the job that Pierre had had and, since she'd decided to carry on his work for him, she took it. One of his duties had been to give physics lectures, so she had to do that too.

Marie's fame, which was greater than ever following Pierre's death, meant the lecture hall was packed with sightseers and she was horribly nervous. There was a huge round of applause when she entered but she didn't take any notice and gave a lecture about the disintegration of atoms (among other things). It followed on from the last lecture Pierre had given and was the first Sorbonne lecture given by a woman.

For years, Marie did nothing but work. She didn't see anyone about anything else and she didn't chat about anything else. Though she looked after her daughters carefully, she wasn't a very fun mother. Fortunately Pierre's dad was around to make up for it.

In 1909, Louis Pasteur's Institute proposed that a special laboratory should be built for Marie to study the medical effects of radium. The Sorbonne was very nervous at the idea of losing its star employee and suggested that it joined up with the Pasteur Institute to build a new Radium Institute consisting of two laboratories, one to study radiophysics and radiochemistry, the other to study the medical uses of radioactivity.

The scandalous scientists

In the spring of 1910, Marie was the same she'd been ever since Pierre died – withdrawn, ill-looking and dressed in black. But, by the summer, she had started to wear white dresses and flowers. The reason was Paul Langevin.

Paul was a scientist – he'd invented sonar and come up with an electron theory of magnetism which Michael Faraday would have loved. So he was ideal for Marie – except he was married. In those days, married men quite often had affairs and, so long as they didn't make them too obvious, no one minded (not even their wives, sometimes). For well-known women, however, it just wasn't supposed to happen. Jeanne Langevin soon found out about the affair and threatened to murder Marie. She also arranged for some love letters between Paul and Marie to be stolen and threatened to publish them.

In 1911, Marie was invited, along with Paul and other top scientists, to an international scientific meeting called the Solvay conference. Marie had a great time, making friends with the even more famous scientist Albert Einstein (who said she had a 'sparkling intelligence'). The conference was fun, but for Jeanne this public appearance of Marie and Paul at the same place – even though they weren't actually together – was the last straw. She published the stolen letters in a paper and there was an outcry; suddenly no one seemed to be on Marie's side. It wasn't just the fact that she had a married lover that people criticized – they didn't like her nationality or her left-wing politics either.

What happened next was about the only thing that could have cheered Marie up – she became the first person ever to receive two Nobel Prizes. This new one was for the discovery of polonium and radium.

But the stress of being persecuted, constant exposure to radioactivity and poor diet were too much and Marie collapsed with a severe kidney infection. It was a year before she recovered, and she was never really well again. She also split up with Paul. She never had another affair, and she never wore white again.

Marie devoted herself to the development of the Radium Institute and, to escape the press as much as possible, she started to travel abroad as soon as she was well enough. In March 1913 she had just the sort of trip she loved, involving both the countryside and science. Albert Einstein and his son Hans met up with Marie and her daughters for a hike in the mountains. Though Albert liked Marie and was impressed with her intellect, on this trip he found her a bit cold. In fact he said she was like a herring. Given that she was more or less on the run from the press at the time, it's probably not too surprising.

Marie's X-cellent idea

In 1914, the First World War began – which meant a complete change for Marie. She said, 'It will certainly be necessary to put science aside and think only of the most pressing national interests.' Which is quite an amazing statement since science always had been a major part of Marie's life and had been all that mattered to her for the last eight years. But for Marie, patriotism was very important indeed.

Paris was evacuated but Marie stayed behind in the almost-deserted city to safeguard her nearly built Radium Institute and its radium. Later, with Paris under threat, she took the radium to a bank in Bordeaux. But what, she wondered, could she do to help the war effort?

Marie was a very determined woman though, and by the end of the war she had established 18 X-ray cars, which she occasionally drove herself. She also trained the nurses for them. One trainee was her daughter Irène, and they worked together for the rest of Marie's life.

By the end of the war, in 1918, Marie was popular again – she'd proved her patriotism and the affair with Paul Langevin was almost forgotten. When peace was announced, Marie made some French flags, stuck them on the Radium Institute and then, finally, started to work there.

But the war had changed Marie – she no longer devoted herself purely to science. To build a better world on the ruins of the old one, she knew political efforts were important too. So in 1922 she joined the Commission on Intellectual Co-operation of the League of Nations, and spent quite a while nagging Albert Einstein to join too.

Other non-science activities were also necessary – though nice and shiny (in fact, glowing in places), the Radium Institute had hardly any money and certainly not enough to buy more radium, so Marie teamed up with a journalist called Marie Meloney, to organize publicity to raise funds. The Maries ended up in the United States on a seven-week tour.

By this time, Marie was dead famous, and everyone wanted to see her and tell her what a really jolly good person they thought she was – in fact she was entertained on her arrival at New York harbour by three different national anthems (sadly all played at the same time). For the sake of the tour, she even made a slight concession to fashion by wearing a hat – the cheapest one she could find.

On the whole, the tour wasn't much fun for Marie (Marie Meloney said she had 'the saddest face I ever looked upon' even before they left Europe). But she did enjoy meeting up with top US scientists and, of course, seeing their labs.

The Maries' fund-raising strategies came in for some criticism; it was obvious that people were far more likely to give money for a cure for cancer than for a bit of pure research into the nature of the Universe by a boffin, even if she did wear a quite nice hat. So, although there wasn't really much evidence that radium could do anyone any good, it was as a curer of cancer that Marie was publicized. This may not have been entirely her fault – people found it very difficult to accept that a woman could be as great a scientist as Marie was, but they were used to the idea of women as healers. Anyway, the tour did the trick and ended with President Harding giving Marie a whole gram of radium for her Institute.

Radium: the awful truth

The Radium Institute was the only place Marie wanted to be. In 1927 she said, 'I do not know whether I could live without the laboratory.' Like Louis' Pasteur Institute and Isaac's Royal Society, she regarded it more or less as her personal property and some workers and students found her cold and dictatorial. But she became more human once she was convinced that new recruits were really into science. Nevertheless, the Institute was a very serious kind of place – in fact it was a lot more like a monastery than Gregor's real monastery was.

Meanwhile, not everyone took radium quite so seriously…

Until 1925, when it became clear that even small doses of radioactivity could kill. This was something that Marie *didn't* take too seriously – she couldn't really believe that something so amazing, that she and Pierre had worked so hard to develop together, and that hadn't killed her after years of exposure, could be really bad. She did introduce blood tests for her workers and precautions like lead shielding, but she remained convinced that the damage caused to living tissue by radioactivity was only temporary – when her workers became ill she sent them to the country, her cure for practically everything.

By 1929, Marie was really ill, but nevertheless she made a second fund-raising trip to the United States, for another gram of radium – but not for her Institute. It was for a new Radium Institute in Poland, run by her sister Bronia. Five years later her daughter Irène, together with Irène's husband Frédéric, managed what alchemists like Isaac had been attempting for centuries – they changed one element into another, using radioactivity to convert aluminium into a radioactive form of phosphorus. The couple received the Nobel Prize, and this was to be the last real satisfaction of Marie's life.

The same year, while working in her beloved laboratory, she collapsed with a fever. She retreated to the countryside, but this time it couldn't help and a month later she died, probably of leukaemia caused by her long-term exposure to radioactivity. Her notebooks are still so radioactive that anyone who wants to look at them has to sign a form to say it's their own silly fault if they become ill as a result.

She was buried with Pierre in Sceaux, on the edge of Paris. Over the coffin, Bronia scattered a handful of Polish soil.

MARIE CURIE
THAT WAS YOUR LIFE
Revolutionized:
physics

TOP DISCOVERIES:
• radium and polonium

NON-SCIENTIFIC INTEREST:
the countryside

Marie had no theory of her own as to where the enormous energy in radioactivity came from. It took one of the greatest scientist ever to discover the amazing truth – Marie's friend, Albert Einstein.

ALBERT EINSTEIN AND HIS LAWS OF TIME

Albert Einstein explained the radioactivity that had made the Curies famous, followed through Galileo's plan to apply mathematics to the Universe, improved on Newton's laws, developed Faraday's ideas of unification, had the patience of Mendel, was a *lot* nicer than Pasteur and liked the seaside as much as Aristotle. And, not only is he the most famous scientist of all, he was also – arguably – the most brilliant.

Albert was born in Ulm, Germany, in 1879. His dad was a rather vague kind of an engineer and his mum was a rather intense kind of an amateur musician. Throughout his life, Albert would be intense, vague and musical too.

Albert didn't take kindly to being educated. He wanted to *understand* why things are the way they are, rather than just being taught facts. When he didn't understand something, he didn't just think 'Ooh how weird… Ah well, I wonder what's for tea?' Not Albert – he got upset and kept on trying to understand until he managed it.

The school Albert went to didn't encourage that kind of approach. The teachers just tried to make everyone learn things by heart, and as a result they and Albert weren't too keen on each other. Luckily, Albert's parents invited a nice brainy bloke called Max round each week and he and Albert talked science. Albert learnt more from Max than from his teachers. Max lent him books to read and Albert rapidly learnt more and more, and got brainier and brainier until…

WE'RE OFF TO MILAN TO START A NEW LIFE. DON'T WAIT UP BECAUSE WE WON'T BE BACK… WELL, EVER, REALLY.

YOU CAN JOIN US NEXT YEAR THOUGH, WHEN YOU'VE FINISHED SCHOOL.

Albert, being the cleverest person that's ever lived, soon sussed out a way to escape from his school and joined them a lot sooner than they had in mind. Once he got to Milan and his parents had recovered from the surprise, Albert dropped another slight bombshell – he didn't want to be German any more. At that time Germany – including its schools – was highly militaristic and Albert hated it. His parents sighed and said OK, and his dad wrote off to Germany to ask that his son be allowed to renounce his citizenship. So, on 28 January 1896, Albert became officially stateless.

Albert had a great time in Italy but he decided the thing to do was to go off to Switzerland to learn more science at a highly brainy place called the Swiss Polytechnic – the Poly, as everyone called it.

The light mystery

Sadly, Albert failed the entrance exams. Shocking isn't it? Perhaps that'll cheer you up next time you fail one. Albert was probably a bit surprised too. Luckily though, the Head of the Poly realized that he had a bit of a genius on his hands and suggested Albert went to a different school in Aarau where he could prepare to have another bash at applying to the Poly.

Albert had a good time at the Aarau school, not least because he was now so intensely brainy that he was ready to get started on sussing out the Universe, which seemed a generally good plan. He asked himself a question:

WHAT WOULD IT BE LIKE TO TRAVEL ALONGSIDE A LIGHT RAY?

There were two ways to answer this question:

BUILD YOUR OWN SPACESHIP

Albert chose the latter, mainly because he had to. It was a very long think indeed – it took him about ten years. For now, all he could work out for sure was that something very odd was going on in the Universe because, for one thing, if he did travel along with a light ray, he would see it as a varying electromagnetic field but one which didn't move along through space. Yet such a thing had never been encountered. It was all rather puzzling.

Albert *did* get into the Poly and he made some good friends, including Marcel Grossman and Mileva Maric.

He studied mathematics, physics and astronomy – a bit. Generally speaking, he borrowed Marcel's lecture notes instead of making his own, being rather busy during the lectures daydreaming and falling in love with Mileva.

After helping Albert pass his Poly exams, Marcel found him a job at the Swiss Patent office in Bern as a patent examiner. His job involved picking holes in the plans sent to the office by budding inventors, so it was nice and scientific and quite fun. Meanwhile, in Hungary, Mileva had a daughter, Lieserl. When she joined Albert in Bern they married, but Lieserl was left behind – presumably she was adopted, though she may have died of scarlet fever. In those days people who had kids when they weren't married were frowned on big time (unlike in Galileo's time when it was just the kids who suffered), and Albert may have thought he'd lose his job if he didn't keep quiet about it. But it was, to say the least, a bit tough on Mileva and Lieserl.

The laws of time

So Albert was settled at last – at least for a while. He was incredibly busy since he gave private lessons as well as working six days a week at the patent office, not to mention having a new son, Hans Albert, to look after, but he was happy with Mileva and they had a reasonable amount of money. It was time to sort out that mystery about travelling at the speed of light which had been bothering him for the last decade. And he solved a few other mysteries of science at the same time too.

① ATOMS (TOO SMALL TO SEE)

②...COLLIDE WITH PARTICLES WHICH ARE TINY

③... BUT VISIBLE WITH A MICROSCOPE

④... ALLOWING US TO WORK OUT THE SIZE AND MOTION OF ATOMS FROM THE MOTION OF THE PARTICLES.

$$\langle x^2 \rangle = \frac{RT}{3\pi Nan} t$$

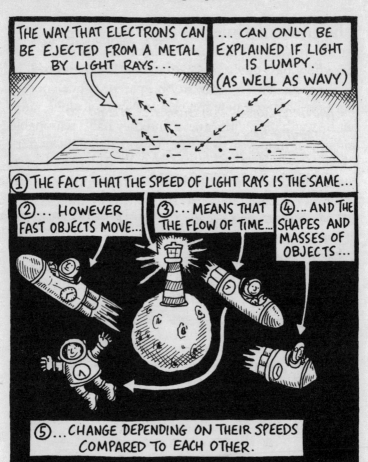

It's hard to say which of Albert's discoveries of 1905 was the most important, but his most famous is relativity. In coming up with it, he didn't do any experiments, make any observations or even do any sums, at least not at first. He just thought out the answer logically – much like Aristotle, except Albert got the right answers.

Once he'd done a few more thought-experiments, the right answers included:

THE RULES OF TIME AND SPACE

- *It's not possible to say that two events happen at the same time.*
- *Moving clocks run slow according to someone they move past.*
- *Moving things shrink according to someone they move past.*
- *Moving things get heavier according to someone they move past.*
- *You can't tell you're moving (just as Galileo always said).*
- *You can't go faster than light.*
- $E = mc^2$

OBVIOUSLY, E STANDS FOR ENERGY, M FOR MATTER AND C FOR THE SPEED OF LIGHT.

The equation $E=mc^2$ says that matter and energy can change into each other, and each lump of matter is equivalent to an enormous amount of energy. To work out how enormous, all you need to do is multiply the amount of matter by the square of the speed of light. Since light is fast enough to go seven times round the Earth in a single second, its square is totally ginormous. $E=mc^2$ explained radioactivity – the energy from the atoms that zapped cancer cells (and Marie too) was being created by the destruction of matter.

SECRETS OF SCIENCE

Einstein's discovery that mass and energy can change into each other revolutionized science. $E=mc^2$ explains how chemical reactions work, how light is produced, why the Sun shines and how atoms form. And it also opened the way for nuclear power stations – and atom bombs.

Over the next few years Albert got several university jobs – as well as a second son, Eduard, in 1910 – and in 1914 he ended up with a university job in Berlin. He wasn't very happy that it was in Germany, but he just couldn't resist the list of duties:

Job title:
Member of the Prussian Academy, Professor at the Friedrich-Wilhelm University and Director of the Institute of Theoretical Physics
Responsibilities:
Turn up at lectures from time to time

But this move was the last straw for Mileva. She and Albert hadn't got on well for some years and after only a couple of months she and their sons moved back to Zurich. In 1919, she and Albert divorced and he married his cousin Elsa.

Four months after Albert had moved to Berlin in 1914, war broke out. Until the First World War, Albert's big interest was physics. He was a kind and tolerant man who hated injustice and militarism, but he wasn't interested in politics. But during the war he started to work for peace as well as for science, organizing anti-war campaigns and joining in protests. He worked *almost* as hard for peace as for science, but not quite – as he said: 'Equations are much more important to me, because politics is for the present, while [the equations] are for eternity.'

The black Sun

The science that was most important to him just then was General Relativity. It was the greatest theory ever developed by a single person, and it explained gravity, allowed the possibility of travelling to the past and knocked the socks off Newton.

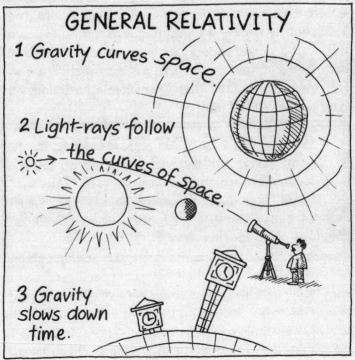

4 A dense enough thing can curve space enough to close it.

5 The Universe might be dense enough to close space.

Albert came up with the basis of General Relativity in 1907, but he needed a lot more maths than he knew to work out a proper theory. With some help from his old mate Marcel Grossman he finally got it sussed, but it was far more complicated than special relativity and very hard to understand fully.

SECRETS OF SCIENCE

General relativity is the tool that scientists use to understand the structure and origins of the Universe and the behaviour of massive objects like black holes. Some think it holds the key to travelling backwards in time too.

What Albert needed next was a big demonstration to show that his theory was really correct. To show other people, that is – he had no doubts about it himself, the theory was simply too elegant to be wrong. And in 1919 he managed it; there was a solar eclipse that year and two expeditions were organized to travel to parts of the world where it would be visible. According to Albert, if General Relativity were correct, the stars would appear to move away slightly from the blackened Sun as it passed close to them in the sky. After a lot of excitement and calculations and worrying about clouds and measuring and so on, the results were all in – and Albert was declared right. (Though it later became clear that the results weren't good enough to be sure, but many other observations have proved him right since.) Almost overnight, he became dead famous.

The lumpy Universe

Albert travelled all over the world talking about relativity, getting a Nobel Prize and meeting up with other scientists. But it wasn't all fun and physics. At the time, Jews were being targeted by right-wing groups in Europe and Albert stood up for them – which made him hated by those groups. They spied on him, tried to blackmail him, paid scientists to say his theories were wrong (or stolen) and seem to have tried to assassinate him too.

Despite these irritating distractions, Albert continued his efforts to sort out the Universe. He was trying to extend relativity into an even *more* advanced version than the General one. He wanted to come up with a 'unified field theory', the sort of thing that Michael Faraday had dreamed of, that would link electricity and magnetism into relativity theory, as he had already done for gravitation. And that wasn't the only science he was busy with at the time – he was also involved in a huge debate about a theory he'd helped develop in 1905: quantum theory.

In 1905 Albert had shown that, as Isaac Newton had always said, light exists as particles which are now called photons (though these particles behave in ways that are much more complex than Newton thought). In fact, Albert realized that the whole Universe is lumpy – that energy as well as matter comes in little tiny chunks. Other scientists as well as Albert developed a whole new science called quantum physics based on this idea and it was highly successful in explaining all sorts of things. Most of the quantum physicists thought that the theory meant the Universe looked like this (although Albert didn't always agree)...

Twentieth Century Physics
THE UNIVERSE: A CLOSER LOOK

1 Light – and everything else – is lumpy, but the lumps behave like waves.

2 It will never be possible to predict exactly what the lumps will do. ✗ *We can't do it, but it's not impossible.*

3 If we had an impossibly powerful microscope, we'd see that very small particles have fuzzy edges.

If we could see such small things, they'd be sharp-edged ✗

Almost all scientists today are convinced that Albert was wrong for a change.

SECRETS OF SCIENCE

Quantum physics is the name given to the weird laws that tiny objects like atoms and their components obey. It has not only explained the behaviour of such objects but also forms the basis of modern chemistry, electronics and genetics.

In the 1930s, Germany was becoming an impossible place for Albert and other Jews to live – many were terrorized, murdered, or had their property stolen. Albert kept speaking up against the Nazis, and it would have been fatal for him to stay in Germany any longer. So in 1933, he and Elsa moved to the USA, never to return.

While in America, Albert continued arguing about quantum theory and working on unified field theory – and in so doing he came up with more amazing science. He also continued to campaign against war. By now he was intensely famous, and popular too, and was offered all sorts of honours including the Presidency of Israel. (Which he turned down – he wouldn't have really known what to do with a whole country of his own.)

In the late 1940s Albert became ill and in 1955 he died, having worked on the unified field theory right up to the night before his death. Half a century later, no one else has completed it.

ALBERT EINSTEIN
THAT WAS YOUR LIFE
Revolutionized:
physics and astronomy

TOP DISCOVERIES:
- theory of relativity
- quantum theory
- proof that atoms exist

NON-SCIENTIFIC INTERESTS:
playing the violin, sailing and world peace

SCIENCE NOW

So now scientists have had a few centuries to suss out the Universe. And this is what they've come up with:

ARTIFICIAL MATERIALS: CHEMICAL ENGINEERING

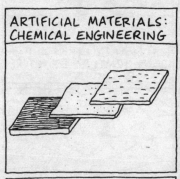

PINNING DOWN REALITY: CALCULUS AND STATISTICS

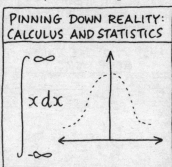

$$\int_{-\infty}^{\infty} x \, dx$$

SAVING LIVES: MEDICAL SCIENCE

PRODUCTION AND DISTRIBUTION OF ELECTRICITY: ELECTRICAL TECHNOLOGY

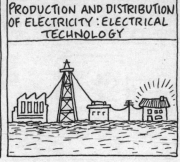

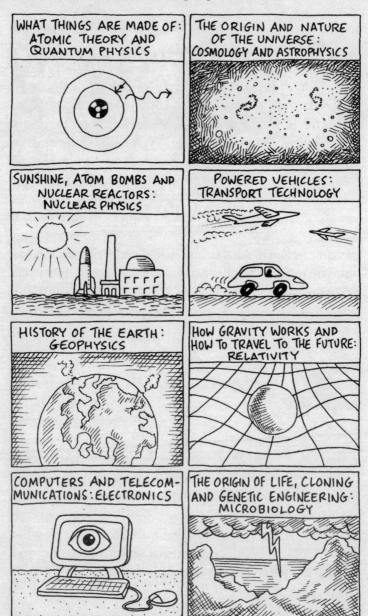

It took so long to get this far because scientists had to be brave as well as clever and to have the time and money as well as the determination to succeed. And they had to be born in the right place and time. Unfortunately, most times and places through history – and many places today too – were just packed with people ready to cut your head off or burn you alive if you didn't believe what they said you should, wiping out those who wanted to go their own way and think their own thoughts, including scientific ones. The freedom to think things through for yourself and tell other people your ideas is unusual, but when people have this freedom it's amazing what they can come up with.

If you're not content just to say 'God did it', the world becomes an incredibly difficult place to understand: stars, spiders, snow – what are they? Where do they come from? How do they work? Suddenly, the world is full of mysteries. But it's also full of clever people determined to understand them. They tried lots of ways and came up with many explanations, and through their struggles the scientific method gradually developed.

Untangling the world is incredibly difficult, but the massive advantage science has over any other approach is that once someone has the right answer, that answer can be *proved* – you don't have to have faith to believe that stars are spheres of glowing gas or that snowflakes are water crystals, you can prove it. To sort out the Universe, all people need is to be allowed to think what they like. Their cleverness, determination and fascination with the world around them will do the rest, given time.

So where will science take us next?

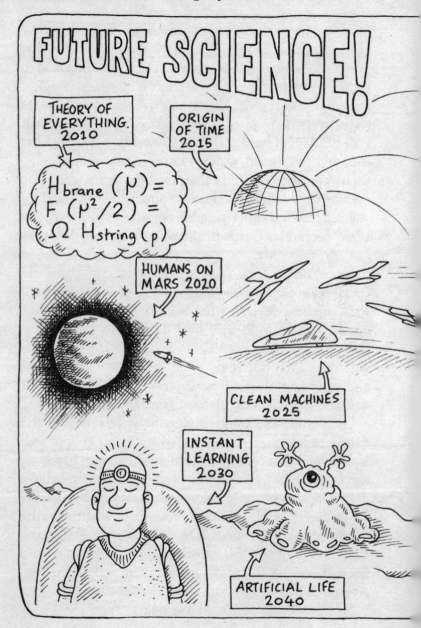

ALSO AVAILABLE IN THE *DEAD FAMOUS* SERIES

Dead Funny ~ Dead Gripping ~ Dead Famous